Annie Sloan

Colorful Living

Aubusson Blue

Calm Harmony

Coco
or
French
Linen
Neutral

Versailles

Annie Sloan

Annie Sloan

Colorful Living

30 CREATIVE UPCYCLING PAINT
PROJECTS FOR YOUR HOME

CICO BOOKS

First published in 2025 by CICO Books

An imprint of

Ryland Peters & Small
20–21 Jockey's Fields
London WC1R 4BW
and
1452 Davis Bugg Road
Warrenton, NC 27589

www.rylandpeters.com
email: euregulations@rylandpeters.com

Text copyright © 2025 Annie Sloan
Design copyright © 2025 Ryland Peters & Small
For photography credits and copyright information, see page 175.

Editor: Sophie Devlin
Art Director: Sally Powell
Designer: Geoff Borin
Production Manager: Gordana Simakovic
Senior Commissioning Editor: Annabel Morgan
Creative Director: Leslie Harrington

10 9 8 7 6 5 4 3 2 1

UK ISBN: 978-1-80065-415-0
US ISBN: 978-1-80065-418-1

British Library Cataloguing-in-Publication Data. A catalogue record
for this book is available from the British Library.

Library of Congress CIP data has been applied for.

Printed and bound in China.

The authorised representative in the EEA
is Authorised Rep Compliance Ltd.,
Ground Floor, 71 Lower Baggot Street,
Dublin, D02 P593, Ireland
www.arccompliance.com

MIX
Paper | Supporting
responsible forestry
FSC® C008047

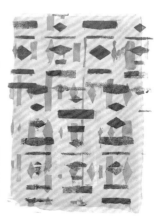

Contents

Foreword

This book is my 27th about paint, pattern, colour and design. It contains 30 brand-new projects, some of which can be completed in just half a day and others over a full day or a whole weekend. They cover many of the techniques I've loved over the years. Whether you favour a rustic farmhouse look, retro 1960s flair or classic English country-house style, I wrote this book for you, especially if you are decorating your home on a budget.

My interest in upcycling began at a young age. When I was a child my father took me to furniture auctions and he would let me bid on small boxes of what were called 'sundries': assorted buttons, broken jewellery, thimbles and so on. I learned that one person's junk is another person's treasure.

Then, throughout college, I clothed myself and decorated my bedroom using items from jumble sales. These were events that happened weekly in church and village halls all over the country. I rummaged through mounds of old clothes, the contents of granny's attic, kitchen paraphernalia and household odds and ends, all on sale for extremely low prices to raise money for local causes. And so when I began setting up my first home, it was natural to

Chalk Paint comes in many hues, from soft neutrals to vibrant shades – see pages 34–35.

Different colours can be layered to add depth, as in this project on pages 100–103.

search secondhand shops for furniture. The pieces were not only affordable, but often sturdily made and, above all, unique.

Having studied fine art at university, I began to combine my love of paint, art and interiors. I became interested in painted furniture of all kinds, from the work of modern artists such as the Bloomsbury group at Charleston in East Sussex to the rustic folk art and fine antiques found in simple homes and grand houses all over Europe and North America. I particularly loved Swedish painted interiors with all their wonderful colours and techniques. All these influences can be seen in my work to this day.

I painted my first piece of furniture, an old wooden chest, in 1977 or thereabouts. Inspired by an early American piece, I created a similar design using artists' acrylics in many colours. However, the paint wasn't quite right for the look I wanted. Many years later, after much research and experimentation, in 1990 I created my own range of Chalk Paint for use on painted furniture (see pages 20–21). My colours are easy to mix together, just like an artist's colour box, so that you can create your own custom blends.

Since then, I've painted a huge amount of furniture and the vast majority of it has been old. I've experimented with many methods and techniques and tried out lots of colour combinations. I developed many techniques to work with the paint and began teaching these in workshops to students and Chalk Paint stockists all around the world. I love guiding people to mix their own colours and make them pop. Although I came from a fine art background, as a painter and teacher it was important to me that Chalk Paint should be easy to use. Everyone has the potential to be creative, even if they think they were not good at art at school.

Uniqueness is a rare quality in today's mass-produced world and that's part of the joy of upcycling. You can completely transform anything: wood, laminate, metal, pottery, stone, ceramics, fabric and even good-quality plastic. In the antiques trade, wooden furniture is often called 'browns'. However, by using paint you can take unremarkable pieces and turn them into colourful and individual items for your home. I hope over the years I've encouraged people to use a lot more colour in their homes and live a more colourful life.

For many of us, painting is also a form of therapy and mindfulness, providing a much-needed escape from our busy daily lives. That's certainly an important part of why I love painting. Being creative is enormously rewarding: the hunt, the planning, the awful moment when you're not sure and then the great moment when it all comes together. The reward of seeing a piece of painted furniture work in your room and how it brings everything to life is so worthwhile. If you are new to upcycling, there is a whole journey ahead of you.

But possibly the most compelling argument for upcycling is that it is simply a very good thing to do for our planet, reducing waste and saving precious resources. Please, please read my chapter on Why Buy Vintage? (pages 12–13) – I want this vital message to get out to as many people as possible.

In short, upcycling is economical, fun, creative, sustainable and good for the soul. What's more, it is the essence of colourful living.

Re-look, rethink, repurpose – and paint everything!

Sourcing Vintage Furniture

Enjoy the thrill of the hunt! Whether you're arriving at an antiques market first thing in the morning, rummaging in a local junk shop or shopping secondhand on your computer, it's the joy of finding exactly the right piece to transform that keeps you coming back for more.

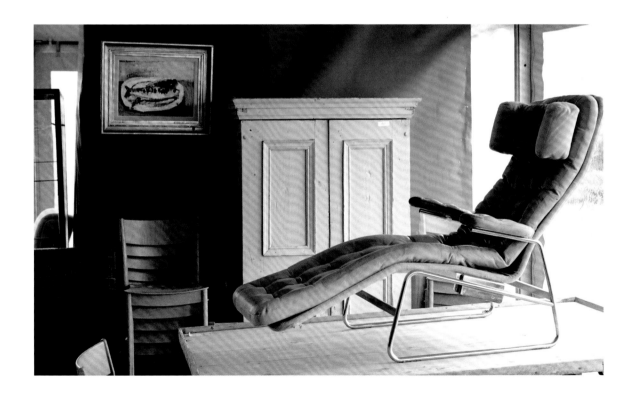

This ornate mirror in imitation Louis XV style could be painted or gilded to give it a new lease of life (above). Architectural salvage can yield a variety of reclaimed items such as these shutters (opposite).

Why Buy Vintage?

Saving furniture from landfill is the rallying cry for this book!

The amount of furniture going to waste is truly staggering. At the time of writing, the Environmental Protection Agency estimates that 12 million tons of furniture are thrown away in the US every single year and the vast majority ends up in landfills. In Europe, the figure is 10 million metric tonnes according to the European Environmental Bureau. Even in Australia, 48,000 tonnes of furniture are discarded at the kerbside per year in the greater Sydney area alone, the equivalent of 800,000 sofas, 1.65 million dining tables, 3.4 million coffee tables and 6.85 million chairs.

Just like fast fashion, in recent years there has been an increase in the production of fast furniture – inexpensive items that may only last for a few years. Synthetic resins, polyurethane foam, chemical dyes, flame-retardant compounds, plastic wraps and other materials make them difficult to recycle, leaving consumers no other option other than to throw them away. These same materials often don't biodegrade or break down quickly when thrown in landfill. They will take decades to decompose, and in the process also leak harmful microplastics and forever chemicals into the surrounding environment.

So, this is a huge and growing problem that we really don't have the space for on our busy planet. It also represents a huge waste of resources – despite the issues with fast furniture, many of the items thrown away are good, solid, well-made pieces that could easily be given a new home. These are the pieces we should be reusing. Instead of always buying new, try to buy secondhand and find ways to repurpose what you have. Remember that anything made of wood, metal, stone, fabric, plastic, laminate and more can be painted to give it a new lease of life.

So, the question is, what's better? A piece built to last that you can sell on or gift when you no longer need it, or a piece that falls apart after five years and is made of materials that are harmful to the environment? For me, the answer is obvious: instead of buying new fast furniture, buy old furniture and paint it.

These pairs of carved doors for sale at a French market date from the 17th or 18th centuries – perhaps they once belonged to a grand château (top).

Old chests of drawers/dressers at an antique market in Avignon, Provence (above). A selection of mirrors and frames from different periods (right).

Where to Shop

First look in your own house for old furniture to upcycle. It may be something you use every day, or a forgotten piece from your shed or attic. Think creatively about how to repurpose things you no longer use.

Next, get familiar with your area and find all the places where secondhand furniture is sold: occasional and permanent vintage markets, charity shops/thrift stores and car-boot/garage sales. You may not find what you are looking for on the first visit, but keep trying and you never know what might turn up.

Online platforms such as Craigslist, Gumtree, Freecycle and Facebook Marketplace are all fruitful hunting grounds where you can find free or very affordable pieces near where you live.

Auction houses have a special place in my heart, although there are fewer than in the past. Attending auctions can take up a lot of time, so you may prefer to look and leave a bid for the things you want, but it does mean you might miss the thrill of the actual bidding. It's worth noting that after every auction sale there is often unsold furniture that is going cheaply because of minor imperfections. There are also great online auction sites such as eBay, although it's now very competitive.

Large house auctions and estate sales are my favourites because you can see a whole house being emptied, from the kitchen drawers to the master bedroom and the garden shed. They offer a great peek into people's lives.

Spotted at a big outdoor market in the English countryside, these wooden frames could be used for art or fitted with mirror glass (top). An artful display of vintage chandeliers (above).

What to Look For

Don't look at the piece as it is, but at the potential. It may be an uncompromising deadly dull shade of brown, and it has horrid handles and some ugly stains, but that's not what you should be looking at. The quality of the construction and the overall silhouette are much more important. I look for well-made, strongly built furniture with a good shape and pleasing proportions.

Most materials can be painted with Chalk Paint, even plastic. If the item you want has been upholstered with an ugly fabric, that could be painted, too. However, there are some exceptions. You can't paint silicone – paint simply rejects it and won't adhere to the surface – and real teak is too oily. Keep this in mind when choosing furniture to paint.

You should also consider how the age and style of the piece will work in your home. For example, I have found that many Art Nouveau and Art Deco pieces from the 1920s and 1930s only really work in the style of that era because their shapes are so strong. You can embrace this with period-appropriate stencils, the right paint colours and copper or silver accents. Similarly, a low-slung mid-century modern cabinet with angled legs is never going to look as though it came from a French château, but you can highlight the features that make it special.

Other styles are more adaptable. Rectangular-shaped furniture with square feet such as the no-frills utility furniture of the 1940s might be perfect for a geometric or colour-blocked design or a simple folk-art motif, as the simplicity of the silhouette allows the paintwork to take centre stage.

Highlight carving and moulding with a lightly distressed finish – see pages 92–95.

The rust effect on this lampshade was achieved using paint – see pages 60–63.

Small objects such as wooden bowls are delightful to decorate – see pages 48–51.

Does the piece have gentle country curves? If so, consider a rustic farmhouse look, perhaps with a very aged and textured surface (see the cabinet on pages 92–95). Is it textured oak? Then don't think of anything too smooth! It needs to be something that makes use of the texture (see the geometric sideboard on pages 84–87). Cabriole legs and some pretty moulding? Then imagine it as a French gilded piece (see the sofa with gilded moulding on pages 128–131).

When it comes to smaller objects, I love finding wooden animals – perhaps tourist souvenirs from Africa – which you can paint in any colour and add your own doodles and squiggles to make them unique. One of my best finds was a pair of large classical busts made of terracotta-coloured plastic, which I bought very cheaply in an outdoor market and then painted to look like ancient stone. They now adorn a console table at my home in France and look magnificent. They look like heavy stone until you pick them up!

Ignore scratches, simple breaks and stains – they can all be fixed and may simply disappear when you paint. However, don't ignore major breaks, as mending can be costly, time-consuming or maybe beyond your skills. I personally don't tend to buy pieces that need significant repair work, as I know I probably won't get round to mending them, but if you're happy to do more than the basics then you can get some real bargains.

It's time to get painting!

Tools and Materials

In every furniture project, the right tools make all the difference
to your work. When you are painting, waxing, stencilling
or colour-mixing, using the best paints and brushes
will mark your pieces out as professional.

Chalk Paint in Florence (above) and Amsterdam Green (below).

Paints

I have designed the projects in this book with my purpose-made paints in mind. As a general guide, you will need larger cans (1l) of paint for large projects and small pots (120ml) for smaller projects and fine details.

Chalk Paint

I invented Chalk Paint in 1990 because I needed a paint for my furniture upcycling projects that was versatile and quick to use. With no need for sanding or priming, you can simply pop open the tin, roll up your sleeves, dip in your brush and start painting. It works on wood, metal, laminate, concrete and more, both indoors and outdoors.

Chalk Paint has a lovely soft matt texture and absorbs wax easily. It has been specially created to be used in a huge variety of ways. You can use it on furniture, fabric, lighting, flooring, kitchen cabinets, tiles and outdoor furniture. It can be applied thickly to create texture or watered down to create a fabric dye.

Chalk Paint is water-based and the colours can easily be mixed to create your own bespoke shades. It requires sealing and protecting with wax or lacquer (see pages 24–25).

Colour to the Foreground

Primer Red

Barcelona

Arles

Château Grey

Oxford Navy

Country Grey

Satin Paint

I designed my Satin Paint for projects involving interior wood and metal. This hard-wearing, soft-sheen Satin Paint differs from Chalk Paint in that there is no need to apply wax or lacquer to protect and finish after painting. It is self-levelling, hard-wearing, beautifully pigmented, simple to use and perfect for upcycling.

Wall Paint

Several of the backgrounds for the finished projects in this book were painted with Wall Paint. As the name suggests, this was designed for use on interior walls. It has a wonderful depth of pigment and provides a soft velvet finish to complement your painted furniture.

Brushes

I have created a range of brushes for painting furniture in a variety of different finishes and styles. Working with bad brushes can be very frustrating and is a false economy. Good brushes with long, flexible hairs allow the paint to flow well so that you can be expressive in your work.

In most of the projects in this book I have recommended which brushes to use, but you can choose a brush that suits the size of the piece you are working on.

Medium Chalk Paint Brush

BRUSH TYPES AND SIZES

Where possible, I suggest you use my range of brushes.

CHALK PAINT BRUSHES
The bristles are strong, yet pliable, and are made of predominately pure bristle with natural split ends, allowing you to paint expressively. They hold a large amount of paint and can also be used for applying wax. Available in Small, Medium and Large.

FLAT BRUSHES
Flat Brushes feature advanced synthetic fibres, which help to produce a smooth, contemporary finish. The brushes are designed to take a large amount of paint and to apply the paint evenly, minimizing brush marks. Available in Small and Large.

CHALK PAINT WAX BRUSHES
Chalk Paint Wax Brushes have been constructed with cutting-edge synthetic fibres, to make applying wax a breeze. They are constructed with a blend of pointed and flagged polyester fibres with cross-shaped bristles. Available in Small and Large.

DETAIL BRUSH SET
One set comes with four brushes: Small Round, Small Flat, Large Round and Large Flat.

Small Round Detail Brush

Clear Chalk Paint Wax (left)

Dark Chalk Paint Wax (above)

Waxes and Lacquers

Finishing Chalk Paint with either wax or lacquer is essential; it will seal your finish for years to come and protect from scuffs and water marks.

Chalk Paint Wax is the perfect complement for Chalk Paint. It adds durability, emphasizes the depth of colour and gives a beautiful mellow finish. It can also be buffed to a sheen. It's really easy to get sensational results – allow the paint to dry completely, then use a Chalk Paint Wax Brush or lint-free cloth to apply the wax. Remove any excess wax with a lint-free cloth. As a very rough guide, you will need one 500ml tin of wax for every 3–4 litres of paint. This will vary depending on how many coats of paint or wax you use to cover a piece, and it's always best to have a little wax left over for touching up. With the lid tightly on, it will last indefinitely.

After adding a layer of clear wax to a piece, you can then apply coloured waxes to alter the finish.

TYPES OF WAX

My Annie Sloan range includes a selection of waxes, which are used in some of the projects in this book:

• Clear Chalk Paint Wax

• Dark Chalk Paint Wax

• Black Chalk Paint Wax

• White Chalk Paint Wax

• Gilding Wax

Chalk Paint Lacquer is a hard-wearing, water-based polyacrylic varnish with built-in UV protection, perfect for high-traffic areas and outdoor furniture. It goes on perfectly clear and dries quickly without yellowing over time. Matt Lacquer provides a matt finish and will slightly darken the colour of the Chalk Paint, similarly to Chalk Paint Wax. Gloss Lacquer gives a light sheen, but is not ultra glossy. One 750ml tin will cover 19 square metres (204 sq ft).

Chalk Paint Wax is a protective coating for all your painted projects, whereas Gilding Wax adds a decorative metallic finish – see this project on pages 140–143.

Other Essentials

For the distressed look or to get a fine finish, you need to be able to sand the waxed surface to reveal the wood or another coat of paint. I have a range of fine, medium, and coarse sandpapers for this purpose. I tend to find using just the fine and medium grades is usually enough, but sometimes move onto the coarser paper if I really want to distress the surface of a piece of furniture.

Always have a good supply of clean, dry, lint-free cloths to hand so you can wipe brushes, polish wax, apply and wipe off paint, and generally use them to clean. I often buy old bedsheets from thrift stores and charity shops for this purpose.

The Annie Sloan MixMat is made from a silicone-like material and holds paint on its surface without the paint running off – this makes it perfect for colour mixing.

These items are not essential, but will be useful for many of the projects in the book:

- Apron
- Mixing stick
- Paint can opener
- Pencil
- Sketchpad
- Scissors
- Craft knife
- String
- Tape measure
- Painter's masking tape
- Blu Tack®

I designed the Annie Sloan MixMat for easy colour mixing (left). Scissors and a sharp craft knife are both useful for cutting out stencils (above).

Living With Colour

Understanding colour theory and how a finished piece will work in a room is part of the skill of painting furniture. This chapter reveals some essential rules about neutrals and complementary colours and how they can be mixed, blended and combined to make your projects a success.

Why Colour Matters

I absolutely love colour, and for me it's essential to have a home filled with a wide range of hues. I'm known for using lots of colours in my work, too – some have even called me the Queen of Colour, which I'm deeply flattered by of course!

I often think of colour in an interior as if it were music. There is underlying rhythm, then the balance of high and low notes, quiet and loud with the occasional crescendo to add drama. This chapter will give you the tools to create a harmonious palette for your home.

A house needs a balance of cool tones that recede from the eye and warm tones that project forward. Painted furniture can be the lift a room needs to give it warmth and interest or a cool statement piece that draws the eye in; or it can be something quietly calming. Consider the colour of your walls, whether neutral, pale, dark or bright, so that you can provide an interesting backdrop for your painted furniture projects.

Sometimes I know exactly the colours to use for a project because I have a particular room in mind. Other times I've started with a piece of furniture with no idea where it will live – maybe it will be sold, or maybe it's just something I love and want to paint! I've suggested Chalk Paint colours for each of the projects in this book, but feel free to experiment with your own combinations as you develop your eye for colour.

In this sketch, a cool blue sofa looks stunning against a wall painted in Primer Red (left). My home in Oxford is a place where I can experiment with colour and pattern (opposite).

Start With Neutrals

Let's start with the idea of an interior with a neutral backdrop and then build on it by adding colours. Although a completely neutral room 'works', it can appear bland and dull. You need some touches of colour outside of the neutrals to give the room life and interest.

The chart below shows all the neutrals in the Chalk Paint range, some warm and others cool depending on their undertones. Any of the warm neutrals on the left can be used together, and the same is true of the cool neutrals on the right. Get to know the full spectrum of neutral tones and choose either cool or warm as the basis for your palette.

Next, add a bit of colour. If you choose Old Ochre, a warm neutral with yellow undertones, as the backdrop, you should combine it with deeper yellows, earthy greens or strong reds. To enhance a cool neutral such as Paris Grey, which has a blue undertone, you should add deep blues and greens. So, can we take this a step further and bring in even more colour?

This painted floor is primarily neutral with French Linen and off whites – see pages 132–135 (opposite). Earthy reds and pinks on the wall and the ceramic urn bring out the warm undertones of the neutral hues.

WARM NEUTRAL These colours may have red or yellow undertones.

TRUE NEUTRAL Pure, a bright white, is neither warm nor cold. It can work with either group.

COOL NEUTRAL The colours in this category have blue undertones.

Country Grey

Old Ochre

French Linen

Coco

Honfleur

Olive

Pure

Paris Grey

Chicago Grey

Whistler Grey

Graphite

Old White

Original

The Colour Triangle

You may be familiar with the colour wheel, which shows the three primary colours (red, yellow and blue) and three secondary hues (orange, green and purple). You mix any two primary colours to make the secondaries. I have adapted this concept to create a colour triangle (opposite) based on the shades in my Chalk Paint collection (listed in the key below).

On the triangle, each primary colour has its contrasting shade directly opposite, for example red with green. These are called complementary colours: in each pair, one is warm and the other cool, and one is primary and the other secondary. Together they make the perfect partnership to use in a room. To help you get started, I have made three neutral paint colours that are mixes of two complementaries with white – see pages 36–43.

If you would like to create your own blended neutrals, the good news is that Chalk Paint colours (except for Graphite, Athenian Black, Whistler Grey and Oxford Navy) don't have black pigment in them. This means that, when you add white, the resulting colour is clean and not grey.

Key to my Chalk Paint colours

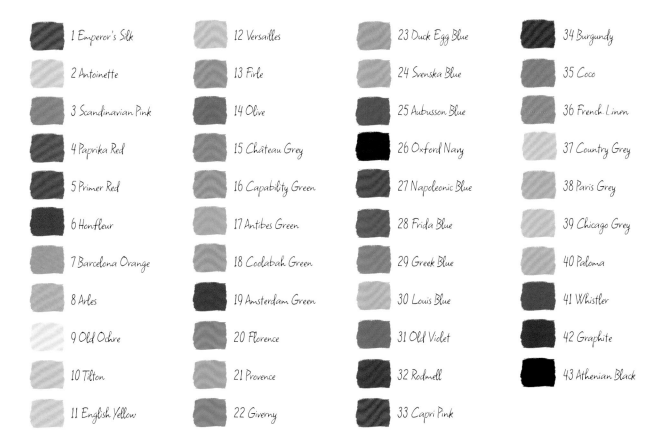

1 Emperor's Silk	12 Versailles	23 Duck Egg Blue	34 Burgundy
2 Antoinette	13 Firle	24 Svenska Blue	35 Coco
3 Scandinavian Pink	14 Olive	25 Aubusson Blue	36 French Linen
4 Paprika Red	15 Château Grey	26 Oxford Navy	37 Country Grey
5 Primer Red	16 Capability Green	27 Napoleonic Blue	38 Paris Grey
6 Honfleur	17 Antibes Green	28 Frida Blue	39 Chicago Grey
7 Barcelona Orange	18 Coolabah Green	29 Greek Blue	40 Paloma
8 Arles	19 Amsterdam Green	30 Louis Blue	41 Whistler
9 Old Ochre	20 Florence	31 Old Violet	42 Graphite
10 Tilton	21 Provence	32 Rodmell	43 Athenian Black
11 English Yellow	22 Giverny	33 Capri Pink	

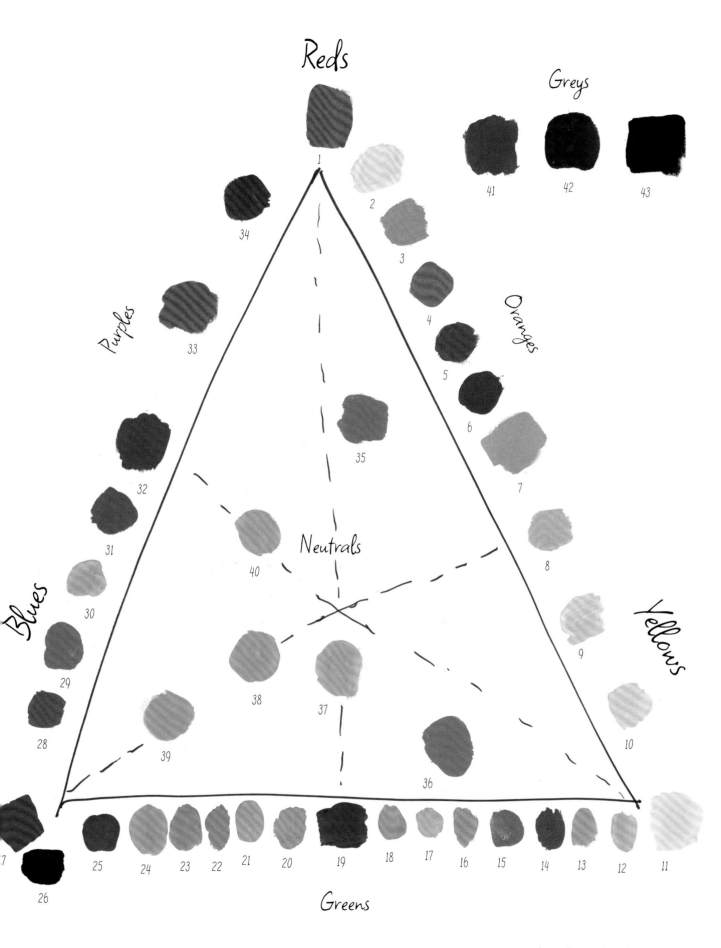

Reds

Greys

Purples

Oranges

Blues

Yellows

Neutrals

Greens

Against a backdrop of Piranesi Pink, the furniture in this hallway has been painted with Chalk Paint in bright Paprika Red and soft Coolabah Green (left).

Using Complementary Colours

Start by learning the three pairs of complementary colours: red and green, blue and orange and yellow and purple. These colour pairs work beautifully together!

Usually as a rule of thumb, you want one of the colours of the pair to be strong and the other more muted, so that they work in harmony and don't compete with one another. Red becomes a deep burgundy, brick red or a pale pink for instance, if used with strong greens. Greens can be muted to become sage, olive or pale.

The other point to remember is that one of the colours (blue, green or purple) will be cool and therefore receding, whereas the other (red, orange or yellow) is warm and projecting. I've made a neutral to work with each complementary pair – Country Grey, Paris Grey and Paloma. These colour pairings and their respective neutrals can be used together on a piece of furniture, or they can form the basis for the palette of an entire room, from wall colours to small decorative objects.

The following pages explore how to use the three complementary colour pairings with their respective neutrals. The neutral can be the backdrop, or alternatively you could choose one of the complementary colours for the background and have the neutral and little additions of the other colour in the room – the choice is yours.

In this bathroom, vibrant Riad Terracotta was used on the walls and pale Louis Blue on the clawfoot tub (opposite).

Complementary Colour Palette: Red and Green

When you use these two colours together in a room, it's usually best not to choose shades of equal intensity. Instead of bright green and bright red, try a soft pink and a strong clear green, or a deep red and a grey-green. You will find you need fewer reds in a room than greens, because reds are warm and projecting. The brighter the red, often the less you need of it. Country Grey is the neutral I have made by mixing red and green with white. Because of its composition, any red or green will look good alongside it. Simple!

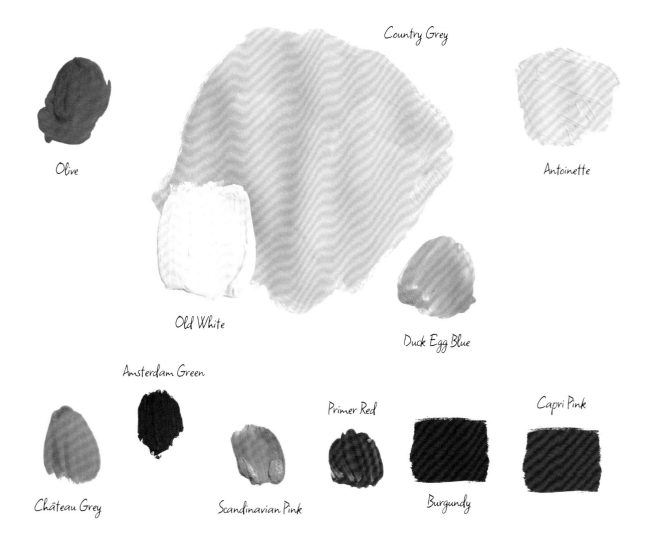

Country Grey

Olive

Antoinette

Old White

Duck Egg Blue

Amsterdam Green

Primer Red

Capri Pink

Château Grey

Scandinavian Pink

Burgundy

Red and Green Complementary Rooms

In these three paintings, I have created three red and green schemes with colour in predominance and neutrals in a supporting role.

This bedroom has Château Grey on the headboard and Duck Egg Blue, a blue-green shade, on the wall (right). To make these cool tones pop, hints of red and pink are used on the lamp, along with whites and Country Grey.

In the second sketch, I have painted a two-toned pale pink wall in Pointe Silk and Piranesi Pink and a neutral floor in Country Grey (above). The furniture and lamp, painted in Château Grey, have been paired with simple white upholstery and a matching white lampshade.

In the third and final painting, we see an Olive green wall with a piece of furniture painted in Emperor's Silk, a deep red (right). You can mix in a deep complementary instead of black to darken any Chalk Paint colour, so I suggest blending the red in places with a tiny touch of deep green such as Florence or Amsterdam Green to give it dimension.

Complementary Colour Palette: Blue and Orange

I mixed blue, orange and white together to make Paris Grey, a beautiful grey-blue neutral that works with all blues from pretty Louis Blue to deep Napoleonic Blue and bright Giverny. It also complements oranges, which include earthy Scandinavian Pink and the rust colours Primer Red and Honfleur. Defining colours is not always straightforward – Primer Red also featured in the red and green palette (see page 38) because it is a versatile shade that can appear either red or orange.

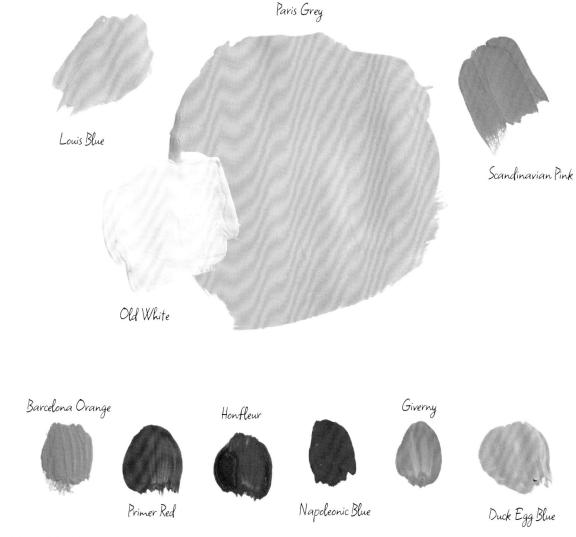

Paris Grey

Louis Blue

Scandinavian Pink

Old White

Barcelona Orange

Honfleur

Giverny

Primer Red

Napoleonic Blue

Duck Egg Blue

Blue and Orange Complementary Rooms

Here we see three ways of combining Paris Grey and its complementary blue and orange hues in interiors, from pale and muted to bold and bright.

This kitchen has Upstate Blue walls and cabinets in Paris Grey, with a deep rust colour on the floor for warmth and contrast (left).

This home office is bold and vibrant, with walls in Riad Terracotta (above). The bureau is painted with Aubusson Blue on the outside and Giverny inside. To soften the effect, the chair and floor are both painted with Paris Grey.

In this more muted scheme, the walls are painted with Old White and Cambrian Blue to harmonize with the Paris Grey floor (left). This cool-toned backdrop allows the Scandinavian Pink chair to stand out.

Complementary Colour Palette: Yellow and Purple

This is the most unsung of the complementary colour pairings in interior design, with the fewest Chalk Paint shades to choose from. However, creamy yellows, ochres, mustards and rich browns work beautifully with fruity damson and plum colours. A soft ochre with lavender, mustard and brown also looks very beautiful. I mixed yellow and purple with white to make Paloma, a neutral that works well with any of these tones.

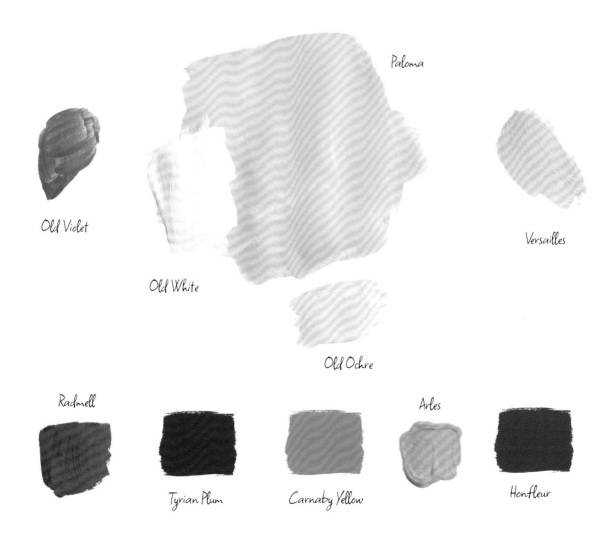

Paloma

Old Violet

Versailles

Old White

Old Ochre

Radmell

Tyrian Plum

Carnaby Yellow

Arles

Honfleur

Yellow and Purple Complementary Rooms

These paintings show three room schemes that use variants of yellow and purple with Paloma and other neutrals, demonstrating how these colours can work together in an interior scheme.

Here, Tyrian Plum walls create a bold backdrop for furniture painted with bright Arles yellow, deep brown Honfleur and their complementary neutral Paloma (right).

Doric Walls, Versailles chair, Pure fireplace
Arles floor with Cream

Doric, a cool neutral shade of grey, is seen on the walls in this subtle scheme, which has a floor painted in Cream with a border in yellow Arles (above). The chair has been painted with yellow-green Versailles and there are Paloma ornaments on the Pure white mantelpiece.

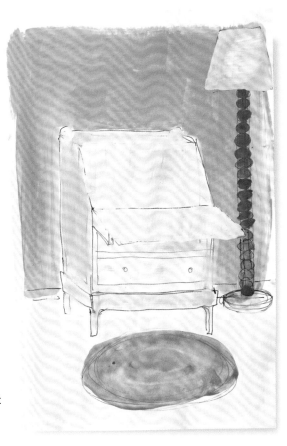

Carnaby Yellow takes centre stage on the walls in this room (right). Painted details in Old Violet on the Paloma bureau stand out against this vibrant, sunny shade.

The Projects

Half Day Projects

If you only have half a day to complete a project, look out
for small, outdated items in your own home or at flea markets:
bowls, jugs, vases, frames, candlesticks and more. Bringing
them to life will give you a fabulous sense of achievement!

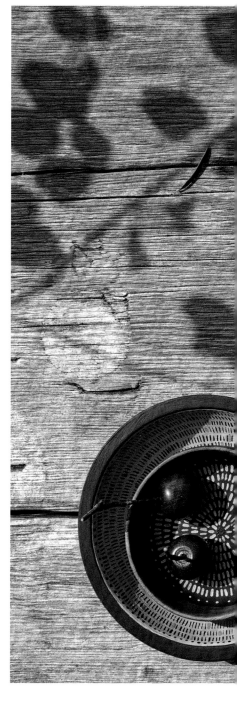

Patterned Wooden Bowls

These bowls were inspired by Cathie Wood of MadeByMeXStudio (@madebymeeex on Instagram). I was introduced to her designs by Tristan Merriam of Doghead Designs, who sells them in his store. Cathie is a treasure hunter and champion of the preloved, who thrills in the unique marks of time on the pieces she sources. I love that her mission isn't just about repurposing, but also reimagining her discoveries, turning the ordinary into the extraordinary.

Cathie's style is so simple but unique, modern and very inspiring. It reminds me a little of the repetitive and dreamy nature of Australian Aboriginal art, but instead of hot reds and yellow ochres, she works with cooling meditative monotones, with the occasional pop of colour.

Wooden bowls can be found in charity shops/thrift stores in all shapes and forms. Here, Victoria and Sophie recreated Cathie's designs, concentrating on the unexpected pop of colour that breaks up the orderly pattern.

It takes time to do it right, but get into the zone and dream away!

YOU WILL NEED

Chalk Paint in Athenian Black, Country Grey and Barcelona Orange

Chalk Paint Brush

MixMat (optional) or containers for mixing

Detail Brush Set

Clear Chalk Paint Wax

Lint-free cloth

This is the bowl I bought from Cathie that inspired me. I painted mine in other colours for a different look.

Athenian Black

Barcelona Orange

Country Grey

1 Paint the bowl, inside and out, with two coats of Chalk Paint in Athenian Black and leave to dry after each coat. We painted the bowl on a MixMat, but this is optional.

2 Paint the inside of the bowl with two coats of Chalk Paint in Country Grey and leave to dry after each coat.

3 For the detailing, pour a little Chalk Paint in Athenian Black and Barcelona Orange onto a MixMat or into containers, keeping the two colours separate, then dilute them both with a splash of water. Using the smallest brush from the Detail Brush Set, begin painting in the details with Athenian Black.

4 Start from the outside and paint your lines in concentric circles until you get to the middle, or vice versa if you prefer, until the inside of the bowl is evenly covered.

5 Use the diluted Chalk Paint in Barcelona Orange to paint the accent details. Leave to dry completely.

6 Seal the inside and outside of the bowl with Clear Chalk Paint Wax using a lint-free cloth.

Patterned Wooden Bowls   51

Brass Candlesticks

Brass candlesticks originated in Europe and the British Isles in the Middle Ages and were commonly used until the middle of the 19th century to hold the candles used to light houses.

These candlesticks were mass produced, so you will come across them in pretty much every flea market or charity shop/thrift store. They have always been popular collectors' pieces, but now they are back on trend in a big way. Painting brass candlesticks is a great way of giving them a new look and adding colour. Chalk Paint adheres to the metal very well and can be scraped off to give a pleasing mix of shiny brass and matt colour.

The treatment Jo used on these candlesticks works equally well to upcycle other beautifully made brass ornaments such as chandeliers, candelabras or wall scones. Depending on the way you apply the paint, your candlesticks can look boho chic or understated and elegant. Before you start painting, use a good proprietary metal polish. Taking your time over preparation is important because you want your piece to look its best.

YOU WILL NEED

Soap and water

Metal polish

Lint-free cloth

Chalk Paint in chosen colours

Detail Brush Set

MixMat

Hairdryer (optional)

Frida Blue

1 Wash and dry the candlestick, then apply the metal polish and buff it to a shine using a lint-free cloth. Apply your chosen Chalk Paint in two coats using the Detail Brush Set and MixMat. You can use a hairdryer between coats to speed the process up.

2 You can either paint your design directly on the candlestick, leaving some areas of brass unpainted, or cover the whole candlestick with paint and then remove it in places to reveal the brass.

3 When removing paint, consider the final look of the piece first. Then use something like the handle of a paintbrush to remove the paint from any curved areas where you want the brass to show through.

TOP TIP Choose the colours depending on what metal your candlesticks are made of. Brass and copper are warm metals, so choose a cool paint colour to create contrast. Silver is a cool-toned metal, so choose a warm paint colour instead.

Textured Vase

I love painting texture in all styles from sleek and modern to traditional and rustic. I've been inspired by studio pottery, rustic country wares, Picasso paintings and folk art from all over the world.

This technique will appeal to anyone who loves paint and texture and it can be used to make anything new look unique and special. The trick is not to be afraid to apply the paint really thickly. Let it dry a bit in the tin to make this easier. Charity shops/thrift stores are full of vases like this one, which has a lovely shape but was otherwise rather dull.

Don't be confined to using this technique to create an old-world effect, as Rachel did here. You can also use it to create something that looks like the work of a modern abstract painter.

YOU WILL NEED

Chalk Paint in Paprika Red, Paris Grey and Graphite

Chalk Paint Brushes

Painter's masking tape

Detail Brush Set

Cardboard/cardstock

Clear and Dark Chalk Paint Wax

Chalk Paint Wax Brush

Lint-free cloth

Paprika Red

Paris Grey

Graphite

1 Paint the vase with two coats of Chalk Paint in Paprika Red, leaving it to dry after each coat. Use masking tape to mark where you want the two colours to meet.

2 Paint the top section with Chalk Paint in Paris Grey using a Small Chalk Paint Brush.

3 A Small Flat Detail Brush will help with any fine details – we chose not to paint the handles of the vase.

4 After you have applied the first layer of paint, start creating the texture. Apply a second layer by stippling your brush on the paint. Continue to stipple the paint as it dries.

5 Use a piece of cardboard to add further texture. Apply more paint in different directions and with different pressure to get a rustic effect.

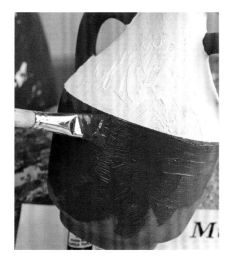

6 Remove the masking tape and apply Chalk Paint in Graphite to the bottom section of the vase using a Small Chalk Paint Brush and Small Flat Detail Brush as before.

7 Repeat steps 4 and 5 on the bottom section to create texture. Using paint that has dried out a little gives you a thicker paint to work with.

8 Leave the paint to dry, then repeat step 5 again to apply another layer of texture. Be careful not to go over the line that separates the two colours.

9 When the piece is completely dry, apply Clear Chalk Paint Wax and leave to dry.

10 Add a final coat of Dark Chalk Paint Wax to give the vase an antique finish.

11 Buff out the Chalk Paint Wax using a lint-free cloth to remove any excess.

English Yellow   Florence   Napoleonic Blue

Murano Glassware

Murano glass comes in many different shapes and sizes, from relatively simple forms to incredibly delicate and intricately crafted designs. In the 13th century, Venetian glass factories moved to the nearby island of Murano to avoid fires spreading through the city and to protect the secrets of glass manufacture. Glassmaking was a highly regarded skill, and makers' techniques were protected by law. As well as its beauty and artistic quality, Murano glass has a romantic provenance.

By the 20th century, Murano glassmakers began to work with artists and designers, elevating glassmaking as an art form. The Arts and Crafts movement of the late 19th and early 20th centuries and the Art Deco style of the 1920s and 1930s helped Murano glass regain its popularity.

Gemma did not find it difficult to source vases and bowls to paint for this project. For example, glass vases used by florists often end up in charity shops/thrift stores. They are fabulous and inexpensive pieces to upcycle.

As you will be painting the interior of your vases, if you want to use them for fresh flowers you will need to put a small jar inside to protect the paint. You can also use the vases for dried flowers. Large bowls can be lit with a tealight inside for a beautiful glow.

YOU WILL NEED

Toothbrush

Chalk Paint in your chosen colours – we used Old White, Burgundy, English Yellow, Graphite, Florence and Napoleonic Blue

Hairdryer (optional)

Detail Brush Set

Chalk Paint Flat Brush

Clear Chalk Paint Wax

Chalk Paint Wax Brush

On the wall: Chalk Paint in Athenian Black
On the shelf: Chalk Paint in Barcelona Orange

TOP TIPS Use a sponge to dab the paint on or scrape away the dry paint with the end of a paintbrush to create an interesting design. Mistakes often bring character to a piece so it can often be seen as a happy accident.

1 The Chalk Paint colour you use first will be the one you see most of, so factor this into your design. Dip a toothbrush into the paint and use your fingertip to flick it across the inside of the vase. Let this first colour fully dry (you can use a hairdryer for speed).

2 Using a Detail Brush and a different colour of Chalk Paint, start to create a freehand pattern on the inside of the glass. Be free with your brush and don't worry about small gaps and uneven coverage.

3 With different sized brushes and in different colours, build up your design. Let each colour dry fully before you move on to the next one to prevent them mixing.

4 Once you are happy with your design, touch up any patchy areas and leave to dry. Seal with Clear Chalk Paint Wax.

Rust Effect Lampshade

For a rustic farmhouse or industrial setting, there is nothing better than a rust technique. The colours are wonderful – the deep orangey-brown works very well in all sorts of interior schemes, especially when teamed with shades of white and with muted greens and blues. The technique looks complex, but it's just a matter of getting the right mix and blend that is largely responsible for that rich rusty look!

It's a signature technique from Jonathon Marc Mendes (@jonathonmarcmendes_paintedlove on Instagram), who created it for us here. Jonathon found this industrial-style pendant lampshade in a secondhand shop. It had a blue enamel finish and looked quite modern and shiny. He wanted it to look old and characterful, rather than new and perfect.

You can use this technique on anything that would rust naturally, especially if it might have come from an industrial or agricultural setting – factory stools, metal tables, planters, vases, even large pieces like old metal lockers and louvred doors. But don't be confined to things that would rust naturally; this technique looks great on many pieces of furniture, modern or rustic.

YOU WILL NEED

Chalk Paint in Graphite, Honfleur, Paprika Red and Barcelona Orange

Chalk Paint Brushes

MixMat

Spray bottle

Bowl or plastic container

Detail Brush Set

Clear Chalk Paint Wax

Chalk Paint Wax Brush

Honfleur

Barcelona Orange

On the wall: Wall Paint in Olive stippled over Wall Paint in Old Ochre

1 Paint the lampshade inside and out with two coats of Chalk Paint in Graphite using a Medium Chalk Paint Brush. Allow ample time between coats for drying.

2 Pour Chalk Paint in Paprika Red onto a MixMat and use your Chalk Paint Brush to stipple a textured coat of Paprika Red over the inside of the lampshade (or see tip opposite). Leave to dry, then repeat on the outside.

4 In a bowl or plastic container, create a wash with three parts Chalk Paint in Barcelona Orange to seven parts water. Then use a spray bottle to saturate the surface of the lampshade with water.

3 While the paint is still wet, pour a little Chalk Paint in Graphite and Honfleur onto the MixMat. Using the same brush with a stippling technique, blend patches of these darker colours into the wet paint so that Paprika Red is slightly visible in the background. Leave to dry.

5 Use a Large Flat Detail Brush to apply the orange wash to key areas such as the top and the bottom rim, continuing to spray the surface and letting the colour drip down the lampshade as you paint.

6 When you're happy with the finished look, leave to dry completely. Seal the inside and outside of the lampshade with Clear Chalk Paint Wax.

TOP TIP I stippled the inside of the lampshade with just Paprika Red to leave a surprising, vibrant pop of colour compared to the external rust effect, but any bright colour would work as well. You could also use Annie Sloan Metal Leaf for fabulous light reflection.

Painted Flower Frame

Finding old frames in junk shops to showcase artworks or photographs
is easy – look for wide frames so the focus is on the picture. I found
a great photo in a 1960s fashion magazine and loved the model in the
simple flower design dress. I slightly enlarged the design and painted it
over the frame. You can also paint old frames with geometric or abstract
patterns to suit your decor – see pages 68–69 for more inspiration.

YOU WILL NEED

Magazine photograph

Scissors

Old picture frame

Chalk Paint in Old Ochre,
Capability Green, Giverny
and Tilton

Chalk Paint Brush

Detail Brush Set

MixMat

Clear Chalk Paint Wax

Chalk Paint Wax Brush

Giverny

Capability Green

On the wall: Wall Paint in Pemberley Blue

Vintage magazines can be a wonderful source of inspiration – this striking photograph dates from the 1960s.

1 Cut out your magazine image and plan out your frame design based on the image you have chosen.

2 Paint your chosen frame in two coats of Chalk Paint in Old Ochre using a Chalk Paint Brush. Leave to dry after each coat.

3 Paint leaves freehand using a Small Detail Brush and Chalk Paint in Capability Green. Leave to dry.

4 Paint the blue forget-me-knot flower petals in Giverny. Leave to dry.

5 On a MixMat, create a mix of Giverny and Capability Green and use this to make little dots on your forget-me-knots. Use Tilton to make a dot of yellow in the middle of each flower.

6 Once dry, seal with a coat of Clear Chalk Paint Wax.

Painted Frames

Here are some more ideas for painted frames, as an alternative to the floral design on the previous pages. You can make your own pictures using found objects, old magazines, vintage handkerchiefs and natural collections of leaves, shells, and feathers – anything that you find inspiring.

VINTAGE HANDKERCHIEFS

Pretty 1950s and 1960s handkerchiefs are easy to find in charity shops and flea markets. I echoed some of the colours and patterns on this hankie using Chalk Paint in Giverny, Capability Green, Original and Capri Pink.

FEATHERS

I arranged some natural-coloured feathers on top of an old water-damaged print. The wooden frame is painted with neutral geometric patterns using Chalk Paint in Honfleur.

MATCHBOXES

This fabulous box frame houses a collection of old matchboxes that I found on an online marketplace. The frame is painted with random dots of colour taken from the matchboxes.

1950S HANDKERCHIEF

This children's handkerchief depicts a picnic scene in bright colours. I painted the frame in circles using Chalk Paint in Aubusson Blue mixed with Giverny so it could be hung in a child's bedroom.

SKETCH

This little sketch of me by my friend Rod Melvin is something I have kept for many years. I painted the frame in Chalk Paint in Duck Egg Blue with an Aubusson Blue edge. Using the head of a nail I then stamped a pattern of dots around the frame using Chalk Paint in Old White.

HANDWRITING COPY BOOK

I created a colourful and busy frame for this old French handwriting copy book. Using watered-down paint I dribbled three colours over the frame, so that the paint collected in puddles.

Raffia Placemats

You will find placemats made of raffia, jute or seagrass everywhere. They last for ages, but after a while they get a bit grubby. Don't throw them away – turn them into beautiful pieces of art.

I first saw this idea from New Zealand painter Jeanie Simpson, who was an Annie Sloan Painter in Residence in 2018. Jeanie showcases her work on Instagram (@jeanius_reloved).

Jeanie painted some old coasters and arranged them into an artwork in her hallway. She said that she loved that with a bit of imagination you can turn almost any old 'stuff' into something useful or fun and avoid more rubbish going to landfill, and I agree.

You can use anything circular for this project – raffia placemats, coasters, old bowls – but the trick is to paint lots of them and preferably in different sizes, too. Jo chose to paint these placemats in a simple target design in bright contrasting shades using a curated palette of colours.

Try to repeat some of the colours across the placemats so that when they are hung, they work together as a family. Instead of targets, you could paint your placemats in geometric shapes, stars, flowers or even African-inspired designs. Getting a good palette of colours that work together is most important, so spend some time getting your colours right.

YOU WILL NEED

Chalk Paint in your chosen colours

Detail Brush Set

TOP TIP Placemats come in different finishes. Some are natural and absorbent, and others have a finish on them; some have a tight flat weave while others are relatively loose. Experiment with using more or less water to get the best finish. Don't fight against the material, just go with it, and let the paint go where it wants to go.

On the wall: Wall Paint in Pointe Silk
On the door: Chalk Paint in Duck Egg Blue
On the chair: Chalk Paint in Frida Blue

Honfleur and Old Ochre   Aubusson Blue and Old Ochre

Dyed Fabric Chair

Charity shops/thrift stores are full of chairs in perfect condition, but with upholstery fabric that may not work with your decor. You might not have the time or skills to re-cover a chair with fabric, but creating your own Chalk Paint dye wash, you can transform your piece.

Brush the Chalk Paint dye onto your fabric in smooth strokes. Think of the process as staining, not painting. Use a paint color that will cover the fabric underneath – it is hard to cover a dark pattern with white or light pastel shades. Natural materials such as cotton and linen will absorb the dye better. This is also the perfect method for adding a pattern, stripes or small areas of colour as I did on this simple little dining chair.

If you want to build up confidence, you can test out this technique out on fabric scraps or any parts of your project that won't be seen first.

YOU WILL NEED

Chalk Paint in Old Ochre, Aubusson Blue and Honfleur

Chalk Paint Brushes

Clear Chalk Paint Wax

Chalk Paint Wax Brush

MixMat

Round objects to use as templates

Detail Brush Set

Iron or hairdryer (optional)

1 Remove the upholstered seat of the chair and set aside. Paint the frame with two coats of Chalk Paint in Old Ochre before waxing with Clear Chalk Paint Wax. Returning to the seat, dip a clean Chalk Paint Brush in water and use it to dampen the fabric all over.

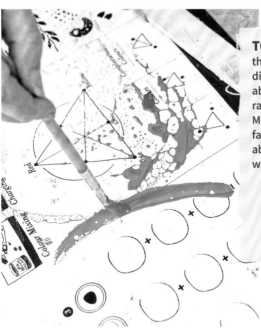

TOP TIP It's difficult to give precise measurements for the ratio of paint to water, as each piece of upholstery is different - the fabric may be thick, textured, and not too absorbent or thin and very absorbent. Use more water, rather than too much paint, and mix up your colour on a MixMat. Test your dye on a piece of fabric first as some fabrics have a barrier on them which means they can't absort dye. Testing first also helps you gain confidence with the technique.

2 The Chalk Paint colour you choose for your dye must be darker than the fabric you are painting – I used Aubusson Blue. Dilute the Chalk Paint with water on a MixMat to turn it into a dye wash. Keep adding water until you have created the colour you want.

3 Dip the brush in the diluted paint and apply it to the fabric. Keep the brush moving to make sure the surface is evenly painted. Don't apply it too thickly, and don't forget the sides. Leave to dry.

4 Apply the second coat to make certain any patchy areas are covered. Leave it to dry. You may need to add further coats if there are still patchy areas. The number of coats will vary depending on the upholstery fabric.

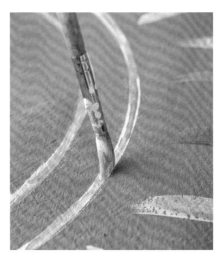

5 Paint a circle using something round, such as a dinner plate, as a template. I used Chalk Paint in Old Ochre mixed with a little water to help it flow easily. Place the template in the centre of the seat and paint around the edge of it using a Large Pointed Detail Brush.

6 Take a smaller round object, such as a side plate, and use it as a template to draw another circle inside the first one with diluted Chalk Paint in Honfleur.

7 Add life to the outer circle by painting diluted Chalk Paint in Honfleur over the top. Paint small radiating lines in alternating Honfleur and Old Ochre around the outer edge of the seat. Heat seal using an iron or hairdryer. Alternatively, you can wax the fabric with Clear Chalk Paint Wax, which will take on a leathery feel when it dries.

Decorative Plates

Old plates are two a penny in charity shops/thrift stores. Turn them into one-of-a-kind decorative art pieces that you have designed and hand-painted yourself. Plan out your design before you start, but let your creative juices flow as you start painting.

Choosing your palette is very important. The colours I have chosen are slightly clashing, secondary and tertiary colours rather than primary colours. This creates a great palette of colours that will all work together.

Clean and dry the plates. Using a Flat Detail Brush, paint your chosen base colour on. Move the brush back and forth to get a smooth finish. If a bright colour is not covering well, a top tip is to add a bit of white to it to make it more opaque. Alternatively, just add more layers of paint.

Paint your design of lines, dots, flowers and arches, starting with your bigger designs. If you go completely wrong, you can wash it off and start again or you can just keep painting over your design until you are happy with the result.

If you leave your plates unwaxed, the design will wash off if you get them wet. Wax or lacquer your plates to provide a more durable finish. These plates are designed to be decorative rather than to use.

On the dresser/hutch: Chalk Paint in Oxford Navy

YOU WILL NEED

Flat Detail Brush

Chalk Paint in your chosen colours

Clear Chalk Paint Wax or Chalk Paint Lacquer (optional)

Chalk Paint Wax Brush (optional)

Reverse Stencilled Chest

This chest of drawers/dresser started out looking exactly the same as every other piece of yellow-orange pine furniture. Probably every house and secondhand venue has something similar that has become virtually invisible. These pieces may appear bland and unexciting, but they can be made to look interesting and unique.

I wanted a simple but strong design for this little chest, as it's solidly built but rather plain. I started thinking about the cut-out paper snowflakes that children make at school. They are made by folding paper, snipping triangular shapes and cutting the corners off the folds. When the paper is unfolded, it has diamond-shaped holes and decorated edges which could be used as a stencil. This idea developed into me looking at cut paper work, particularly from Eastern Europe. I liked the simple symmetry of their flower designs, so I folded a rectangle of paper and drew half flower, stem and leaf designs to make a daisy and two tulips (see page 170).

To give this simple, carefree design a sense of cohesion, I used only two Chalk Paint colours (Paprika Red and Capability Green) for the base coat and mixed them to make a third colour, a strong khaki neutral. Old Ochre was painted over the drawers and the paper cutouts. The base coat is revealed when each stencil is removed.

Plan out your design before starting. As you can see from my sketches, I drew a design and then changed the colours on the actual project.

Capability Green

Paprika Red

Old Ochre

TOP TIP The stronger the paper or cardboard, the longer your stencils will last. You can varnish them so they last longer.

1 Remove the drawer handles, then paint the whole frame and the bottom drawer with Chalk Paint in Paprika Red using a Chalk Paint Brush. Paint the top drawer with Chalk Paint in Capability Green. On a MixMat, create a blend of the two colours and use this to paint the middle drawer. Paint the drawer handles in the same colours as their respective drawers. Leave to dry.

2 If you want to copy our stencil design, use the templates in this book (see page 170), using a photocopier to change the size if you need to. Take a piece of cartridge paper or cardboard, fold it in half and draw round the flower template or create your own design. Using scissors or a craft knife, cut out the design while it is still folded in half. Open it up to reveal the complete stencil.

3 When you have cut out all the stencils, attach them to the front of the top drawer using Blu Tack®. Make sure they are evenly spaced across the width of the drawer.

4 Paint over the stencils carefully with Chalk Paint in Old Ochre using a Small Flat Brush. Remove the stencils quickly, as you don't want them to stick to the surface.

5 Repeat steps 3 and 4 on the other two drawers. Leave to dry, then reattach the painted drawer handles and finish by applying Clear Chalk Paint Wax all over using a Chalk Paint Wax Brush.

Full Day Projects

Painting a piece of furniture from start to finish in a day is so rewarding. Begin with the planning and first coats of paint, and soon you will be setting up your finished project in its new position in your home.

Aubusson Blue   Giverny

Geometric Sideboard

Geometric shapes can be seen on many pieces of traditional painted furniture, particularly those from Europe. There are a huge number of geometric designs to work from, so look for inspiration from ancient Roman, medieval or Victorian tiles.

This clever piece is made by creating overlapping circles using a glass lid from a saucepan as a template, which allows you to see your design as you work on it. It was inspired by the work of The Art Of Pátina Antiques (@the.art.of.patina.antiques on Instagram), a studio based in Spain that creates all sorts of different patterns and patinas on furniture for restaurants, hotels and houses.

Keep the pattern simple and give it texture to deconstruct and soften it a little. This piece is oak, which has a tremendous grainy texture that makes it hard to make a crisp edge, so the end result is irregular and full of character. Sanding it afterwards to reveal the paint underneath adds to the rough, aged look. I love that covering the whole piece with the design is a bit like wrapping it with fabric – it allows you to see the piece as one cohesive whole.

YOU WILL NEED

Chalk Paint in Pure, Giverny and Aubusson Blue

Chalk Paint Brush

Pencil and paper

Long ruler

Glass saucepan lid

MixMat

Detail Brush Set

Eraser

Clear Chalk Paint Wax

Chalk Paint Wax Brush

Sanding Pads

On the wall: Wall Paint in Olive

On the skirting/baseboard: Chalk Paint in Olive and French Linen

On the floor: Satin Paint in French Linen

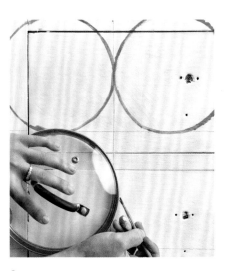

1 Paint the piece using two coats of Chalk Paint in Pure and leave it to dry while you plan out your design. You can copy our drawing or create your own. Whatever you choose to do, sketch out the design on a piece of paper first so that you feel confident before you start painting.

2 Measure the diameter of the saucepan lid. Its size dictates the size of the grid you need to draw on your piece – this lid is 16cm/6¼in across, so our grid is 16cm/6¼in square. Start from the centre point of your piece and mark out a grid pattern using a pencil and ruler.

3 On the MixMat, create a Chalk Paint blend of Giverny and Aubusson. Position the saucepan lid so it fits in the middle of the first square of the grid and paint around it using a Small Detail Brush. Repeat in each square of the grid, then leave to dry.

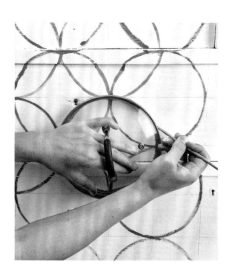

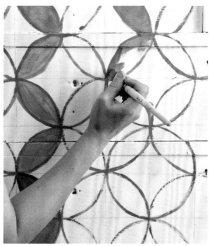

4 Divide each of the original grid squares into quarters – ours were divided into 8cm/3⅛in squares. Reposition the saucepan lid so it is one square to the left and one square down from the first circle you drew. Draw around the lid to create the pattern of overlapping circles.

5 Fill in the areas where the circles overlap using a Large Flat Detail Brush. Don't worry too much about the colour being uniform – it's nice to have a little variation.

6 Using the pencil grid as a guide, fill in half of the central area of each circle as shown. Leave to dry.

7 Load a Small Flat Detail Brush with the blue paint mix and, with a swirling movement, create a small half-circle close to the middle of each larger circle on the Pure background. The grid will guide you.

8 Repeat step 6 to complete the small circles using Pure on the blue blended background. We painted the top of the piece in a wash of the blue paint mix, but you could continue the design on the top if you prefer. Leave to dry.

9 Remove the pencil marks using an eraser, then wax the whole piece with Clear Chalk Paint Wax and leave to dry. Sand back the piece using a coarse Sanding Pad to give it more of a textured, aged look.

Blended Tall Armoire

Many years ago, one of the first pieces I painted with my new Chalk Paint was a big French armoire that I had in my shop in Headington, in Oxford. It was a treasured piece which I painted using this blended technique in Old Ochre and Château Grey, with Emperor's Silk inside. I imagined it standing in an 18th-century French boudoir, complete with white petticoats and chandeliers. Trés decadent!

Eventually it found a happy buyer, but the piece had hit the spot for me and ever since I have wanted to recreate the same colours and blended technique but hadn't found the right piece or time to do it.

Finding this tall armoire gave me the opportunity. It's a typical French piece – you see them used in kitchens and restaurants to store plates and platters. It had a good flat front with curvy moulding and plenty of surface area so was perfect for this soft cloudy look and it also had an open top shelf to show off the contrasting bright deep red of Emperor's Silk.

YOU WILL NEED

Chalk Paint in Emperor's Silk, Old Ochre, Original, Arles, Pure and Château Grey

Chalk Paint Brushes

MixMat

Clear Chalk Paint Wax

Chalk Paint Wax Brush

Emperor's Silk

Old Ochre

Château Grey

On the wall: Wall Paint in Old Ochre
On the skirting/baseboard: Satin Paint in French Linen

1 Paint the inside of the piece with two coats of Chalk Paint in Emperor's Silk. Paint the outside with two coats of Chalk Paint in Old Ochre using a Chalk Paint Brush. While the second coat of Old Ochre is still wet, start to paint over it with a coat of Original, moving the paint in all directions to blend it out evenly all over the surface.

2 Use a MixMat to mix the three colours in various combinations, using Old Ochre (the medium tone) as the main colour. Add Pure for some highlights, blending it together while everything is still wet.

3 Now add some Arles, working it into the Old Ochre at first and then using it on its own to bring depth. Keep the main colour as Old Ochre, with just hints of the white and deep yellow shades.

TOP TIP As the paint dries, hold the brush upright and use the tip to feather the paint, keeping it moving all the time. This barely-there movement will blend the colours and prevent brush marks.

4 On the MixMat, blend together Chalk Paint in Old Ochre and Château Grey. Work this mixture into the still-wet paint around the indented mouldings to add some depth.

5 Leave the paint to dry completely, then apply a coat of Clear Chalk Paint Wax using a Chalk Paint Wax Brush.

Distressed Country Kitchen Cabinet

The country farmhouse look is ever-popular, as it's undemanding and relaxed. I was on the lookout for something that had some carving or shape and texture to it, which I could paint in this style.

This is a wooden piece made, I think, from old timber with tin tiles on the doors. It would be great in a country kitchen with clean, simple cabinetry in smooth white and this cabinet in a gentle two-colour distressed finish.

If there's one technique I return to time and again, it's the two-colour distress method I developed when I first created Chalk Paint. In just a few simple steps you can create a gentle or very strong and characterful effect. Make it your own with your choice of colours and the amount of sanding you go for. Like uncovering layers of paint on an old piece of furniture, this effect gives the illusion of paintwork that has been enjoyed for decades. But instead of waiting generations, you can achieve this vintage look in the matter of hours.

Although I chose a muted traditional neutral palette for my country kitchen look, you can be quite playful with your colour choice, perhaps using something quite bright as a base coat.

YOU WILL NEED

Chalk Paint in Country Grey and Old White

Small Chalk Paint Brush

MixMat

Clear and Dark Chalk Paint Wax

Small Chalk Paint Wax Brush

Sanding Pads

Lint-free cloth

Country Grey

Old White

On the wall: Wall Paint in Pointe Silk
On the skirting/baseboard: Chalk Paint in Old Ochre

1 Paint the cabinet in two thick coats of your base colour of Chalk Paint in Country Grey using a Chalk Paint Brush and a MixMat. This piece was quite rough, but if yours is smooth, move the brush in every direction to create texture. Our brushes are designed to hold lots of paint to help with this. Leave to dry.

2 Paint a thinner coat of Chalk Paint in Old White over the whole cabinet to make it easier to sand through to the base colour.

3 Once dry, apply Clear Chalk Paint Wax to your piece, working it into the surface using a Chalk Paint Wax Brush.

4 Once the wax is dry to touch, but hasn't hardened, you can start sanding. Using Sanding Pads, remove the top coat of paint to reveal the colour beneath. Start with a coarse pad and move down to medium and then fine grade. For the most authentic distressed effect, concentrate on edges and corners – or any areas that will naturally see wear and tear. You may even want to sand all the way back to the original surface in some places.

5 To further emphasize the shape and texture of your furniture, apply Dark Chalk Paint Wax using a clean Chalk Paint Wax Brush.

6 Smudge the wax with a cloth until you are happy with the the look of your piece.

TIP If some areas are too dark, you can adjust them by repainting them in Old White Chalk Paint and rewaxing in Clear Chalk Paint Wax.

Distressed Country Kitchen Cabinet 95

Dragging Technique on a Door

Dragging is the name of a classic 18th-century decorative paint technique. It's a simplified version of wood graining in which a dry brush (or other tool) is pulled through wet paint, producing fine, blurry and broken stripes with the base coat showing through. Colours are traditionally close in tone and hue.

This technique returns to popularity every now and again when people remember how chic and elegant it is. I dragged many doors when I started out in the late 1980s and early 1990s and I still think it's a brilliant way to make a boring door look interesting and aged.

Original is a soft white that is not too stark and it works with French Linen to create a beautiful neutral look. On this door Sophie used the same colours all over, although traditionally lighter or darker tones would sometimes be used on the panels to give more depth. You could use Chalk Paint to drag over a Satin Paint base, but you would have to wax the door afterwards.

It is essential that you paint the door following the steps on the sketch. Start on the smallest panel first; your speed will improve with practice.

YOU WILL NEED

Screwdriver

Satin Paint in Original and French Linen

Large Flat Brush

MixMat

Wall Paint Brush

Wet cloth

French Linen

Original

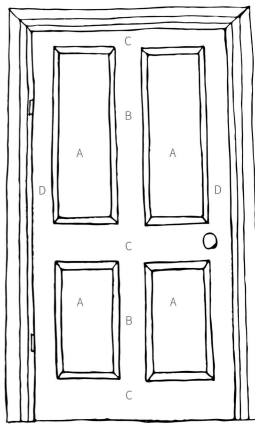

TOP TIP If you find the paint drying too fast, use a damp cloth over the whole area to keep it wet enough to work with. In very hot climates, you may want to put a retarder in the paint to extend the drying time further.

1 Remove any door furniture using a screwdriver. Take a Large Flat Brush and paint the whole door with Satin Paint in Original, then leave it to dry. Paint the door panels (A) with Satin Paint in French Linen. Don't overload the brush; a small amount of paint will go a long way. You can wipe off excess paint on a MixMat.

2 To create the dragging effect, you will need a brush with lots of coarse wide bristles – we used a Wall Paint Brush. Working quickly while the Satin Paint in French Linen is still wet, pull this brush through the paint to create a striped woodgrain effect. Try to pull down all the way from top to bottom in one single stroke.

3 Use a wet cloth to wipe the paint off around the edges of the panels. Sometimes you might have to wipe off all the paint in a particular area and try again, if it looks too inconsistent.

4 The three horizontal segments across the door are called the top, bottom and middle rails. On the vertical panel that separates the left and right panels (B), paint and drag from the top rail to the middle rail and then wipe away the excess paint on both rails in neat horizontal lines.

5 On the lower half of the vertical panel, paint and drag from the middle rail to the bottom rail. Wipe off the excess paint again.

6 Open the door and paint the three rails (C), then drag the paint horizontally using the same technique. Clean the paint off in a neat line where it meets the stiles (D), which are the narrow vertical segments on either side of the door panels.

7 Paint the two stiles and drag the paint vertically as before. Leave the door to dry before replacing the door furniture.

Primer Red

Aubusson Blue

Scandinavian Pink

Palette Knife Colour Layering

YOU WILL NEED

Chalk Paint in Primer Red, Aubusson Blue, Florence, Giverny, Scandinavian Pink and Country Grey

Small Chalk Paint Brush

Palette knife

MixMat

Clear Chalk Paint Wax

Chalk Paint Wax Brush

A palette knife is a small, blunt blade, which comes in various shapes and is used by artists to move paint around on a canvas. It's similar to using a piece of card but is easier to control, especially on furniture.

Palette knife colour layering is a signature technique of Tristan Merriam of Doghead Designs (@dogheaddesigns on Instagram). He's turned it into a great technique for creating texture by scraping and layering the paint.

Choose three or four colours and test beforehand to work out if they not only look good alongside one another but also if they get mixed together – for instance, if you chose a yellow and a blue, they combine to make green. Choosing a neutral as one of your colours will help to harmonize your palette.

We had this piece in our furniture collection but had never found a use for it. It's a small mid-century low side table, which was crying out for some love!

On the wall: Wall Paint in Cambrian Blue

On the skirting/baseboard: Chalk Paint in Aubusson Blue

1 Apply two coats of Chalk Paint in Primer Red and leave to dry after each coat.

2 Using a palette knife, start with the darkest shade, Aubusson Blue, and apply smoothly across the piece. Let it dry.

3 Combine Florence and Aubusson Blue on a MixMat and apply in the same way.

4 Combine Aubusson Blue and Giverny and apply in the same way. You are working from the darkest colours to the lightest.

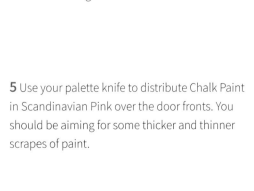

5 Use your palette knife to distribute Chalk Paint in Scandinavian Pink over the door fronts. You should be aiming for some thicker and thinner scrapes of paint.

6 A blend of Country Grey, Aubusson Blue and Florence creates a mixture of lighter tones.

7 The first layers should be quite even but the final layers should be more random.

8 When the piece is dry, seal with a coat of Clear Chalk Paint Wax.

Potato Printed Bedside Table

Block printing using potatoes is a fabulous technique. You don't have to be able to draw to create a stunning effect. Anyone can cut shapes out of a potato and achieve wonderful results. This project combines a good basic potato print with the sophistication of Italian Baroque design.

I love the charming little Tuscan landscape scenes made from colourful inlaid marble shapes that you see on fancy and very expensive Italian furniture. The technique is called pietra dura, which means hard stone. The outlines of the houses, trees and hills are simplified and a little blocky, so I thought they would good to paint using potatoes to make the shapes. I've done it several times before and I know it's a delight to use this technique.

I found this little bedside table/nightstand in France and brought it back to my studio in Oxford. I painted it a few years ago for a photoshoot, but it was due for a refresh. I love the shape of the piece and it has a nice little panelled front, which is perfect for this project.

Before I started painting, I planned out the design for my landscape. I decided on the colour palette and drew some simple tree and house shapes to use to cut out my potato block prints.

I chose my colours inspired by the marble hues in the original Italian furniture. The uneven print is perfect for a marble effect and looks surprisingly sophisticated for something made with a potato!

YOU WILL NEED

Chalk Paint in Graphite, Olive, Paris Grey, Old Ochre, Original, Arles, Paprika Red and Whistler Grey

Chalk Paint Brush

Detail Brush Set

MixMat

Wooden cutting board

Potatoes

Sharp kitchen knife (not serrated)

Paper towels or rags

Pencil or felt-tip pen

Craft knife

Paper

Clear Chalk Paint Wax

Chalk Paint Wax Brush

TOP TIP When creating your design, you can't do anything fussy or it just won't work. The shapes need to be quite loose. The wonkiness is part of the charm of this block printing technique. Use the sketch here and replicate my design or create your own landscape.

Graphite   Paprika Red

1 Paint the whole piece using Chalk Paint in Graphite and leave it to dry. You could use Satin Paint as an alternative.

2 Paint it smoothly; you don't want any texture.

3 Paint the background for the design using simple lines. Use a pointed Detail Brush and paint a sweep of Chalk Paint in Olive, a mid-tone colour.

4 Now use Chalk Paint in Paris Grey. Mix the paint with a little water on a MixMat so it is easy to paint on your piece. Don't worry if you get paint on the moulding.

5 Create a mix of Chalk Paint in Old Ochre and Original with a tiny bit of Chalk Paint in Arles, then use this to paint the sky.

6 If the colours run into each other, don't worry; simply blend them together.

7 Take a cutting board and start to make your potato shapes by cutting your potatoes in half with a sharp kitchen knife to get a clean edge. Get rid of any excess water by dabbing the exposed surface with a paper towel or rag.

8 Draw each of the shapes you have planned out for your landscape on the exposed surfaces of the cut potato halves using a pencil or felt-tip pen.

Potato Printed Bedside Table   107

9 Cut around each outline using a craft knife to leave a relief shape (a raised area). Be careful of your fingers as it can be hard to see what you are doing. Save the offcuts for later.

Olive and
Old Ochre

Paris Grey

Olive and
Old Ochre

Arles

Olive

Whistler Grey

10 Dab some blobs of paint in Chalk Paint in Olive onto the MixMat and use a Detail Brush to cover one of the tree shapes in paint. Make sure there is paint over the whole shape.

11 Use the potato to make some practice prints on paper. Press down quite hard to get an even print.

I painted a slightly different landscape on the side of the piece, so that it looks appealing from all angles.

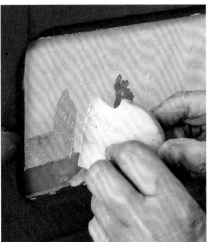

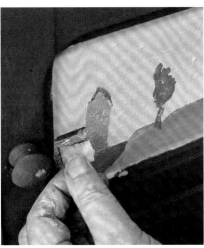

12 When you have mastered the technique, print the trees directly onto the painted background.

13 Add the house shapes using Chalk Paint in Arles, Paris Grey and Old Ochre.

14 Use small offcut slivers of potato to add details: roofs in Paprika Red and windows and doors in Whistler Grey. Fill in any gaps with a bit of hand painting. Leave to dry, then wax your piece with Clear Chalk Paint Wax.

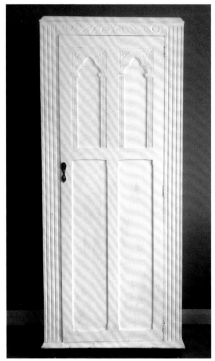
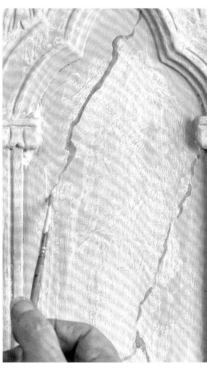

Frottaged and Marbled Wardrobe

YOU WILL NEED

Chalk Paint in Graphite, Old White and Country Grey

Chalk Paint Brushes

Clear Chalk Paint Wax

Chalk Paint Wax Brush

MixMat

Newspaper – make sure you have enough!

Detail Brush Set

I am using two techniques on this piece; frottage, which gives an aged texture and patina, and then marbling, which simulates the more refined look of stone. To show both dark and light marble effects, I painted the wardrobe using Chalk Paint in Graphite and Old White.

Frottage is a wonderful technique that I discovered 30 or more years ago when trying to paint large areas quickly. I often used to cover my floors in thin plastic sheeting to protect them and inevitably they would sometimes rub against the wet paint on the walls. The results I found interesting, although a little too strident.

I experimented and discovered that newspaper was a little more forgiving and subtle. I am still rather obsessed with the way frottage, using the right colours, can turn into marble with a few simple painted marks.

Facebook Marketplace, where I found this wardrobe/armoire, is a great place for finds. I liked the gothic mouldings and columns, which I knew would lend themselves well to these frottage and marbling techniques. You might notice it has a piece missing. Imperfections are common when you buy secondhand. Don't worry, it's part of the joy of upcycling!

Graphite   Country Grey

frottage

1 The wardrobe/armoire has been painted in Chalk Paint in Graphite on the outer edges and Old White on the doors. Apply Chalk Paint Wax.

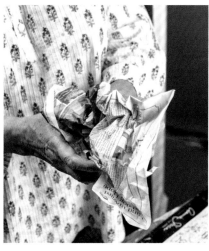

2 You need to work quickly, so prepare enough newspaper to cover your piece before you start. Crumple up the newspaper and then open out the sheets, ready to start frottaging.

3 On a MixMat, dilute Chalk Paint in Country Grey with enough water to make it translucent when you apply it to the waxed Graphite paint. It should be the consistency of single cream/light cream.

4 Paint a thin wash of the diluted Chalk Paint over a small portion of the waxed Graphite painted surface.

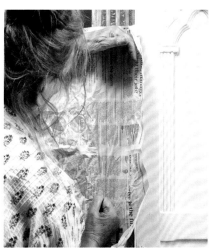

5 Spread the crumpled newspaper over the wet paint and rub it a few times, before peeling it back to reveal a wonderful aged patina. Repeat to cover all the Graphite paint.

6 Repeat steps 4 and 5 on the areas painted in Old White. You will see uneven and blotchy paint, some flat bits, some textured and some stripped back to the first colour – all part of the magic of this technique! Leave to dry.

marbling

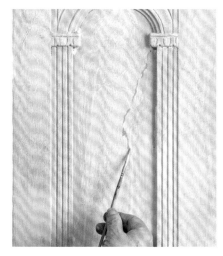

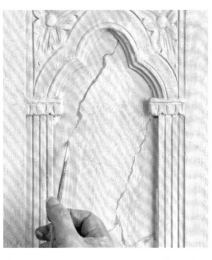

7 On the MixMat, create a Chalk Paint mix of one part Graphite to one part Country Grey and add a bit of water to make the paint flow nicely. Use a Fine Detail Brush to paint a marble effect on the Old White door panels. Hold the brush perpendicular to the piece and let it fall down, marking the door with paint as you do so.

8 Twist the brush to create the effect of finer and thicker veins. Allow the brush to do the work for you. Work from the edges and create shapes that look like shards of shattered glass.

9 If there is an area where the Country Grey colour is too strong, you can soften the lines by feathering over them using a Chalk Paint Brush before the paint dries. Some lines should be darker and some lighter.

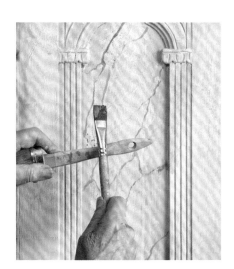

10 Flick little spots of paint over the top of the lines using a Detail Brush and smudge them in to mimic the cloudiness of marble.

11 Markings on marble aren't all the same colour, so go over some of the lines and make some parts darker than others. When you are happy with the look, leave the paint to dry and then wax the whole piece using Clear Chalk Paint Wax.

Old Violet   Greek Blue

Tetra Pak® Stencilled Trunk

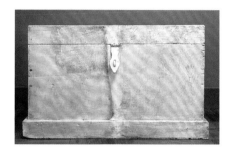

YOU WILL NEED

Craft knife

Cutting board

Clean, empty Tetra Pak® cartons

Shaped objects to draw around
(tape reel, paint pot lid, bottle lid)

Black ballpoint pen and metal ruler

Chalk Paint in Chicago Grey, Oxford
Navy, Old Violet, Greek Blue and
Old Ochre

Medium Chalk Paint Brush

Chalk Paint Roller

Hairdryer (optional)

Clear Chalk Paint Wax

Chalk Paint Wax Brush

On the wall: Wall Paint in Pointe Silk

*On the skirting/baseboard: Chalk Paint
in Old Ochre*

This piece has given me a great deal of satisfaction as I'm making
my stencil from something that would normally be thrown away
and re-using an old piece of furniture to give it a new lease of life.

Every day most of us use something made of Tetra Pak®, such as cartons
for milk, soft drinks, juices and soups. These are typically made of about
70% paperboard, 25% plastic and 5% aluminium. Tetra Pak® cartons
are recyclable, but don't throw them away – they make fantastic stencils!

Stencils used to be made of cardboard/cardstock but nowadays they
are more often made of plastic. Reusing Tetra Pak® cartons is an eco-
friendly alternative – they are waterproof and easy to cut into shapes
with a craft knife or scissors.

This design was inspired by simple abstract, angular and geometric
shapes associated with the Bauhaus, the influential modernist German
art and design school that existed from 1919 to 1933. The piece of
furniture is an old trunk that had been used probably at one time
in a garden shed, so the outside wood was a little rough and uneven.
The random design suited the old wood and gave it character.

TIPS AND TRICKS You can duplicate your stencils by drawing
around them on another sheet of Tetra Pak® – this is helpful if you're
using multiple colours. When the final piece is dry, use a detail brush
to touch up any mistakes or just re-stencil over the top to create the
look you're after.

1 Start by making your stencils. Using a sharp craft knife and a cutting board, carefully open the Tetra Pak® cartons along the seams and cut off the lids. Flatten out the material so that the silver side is facing up. Draw around your chosen objects with a ballpoint pen (or draw lines with a metal ruler) to create circles, squares, rectangles and triangles, then use the craft knife to cut out the shapes. Use several cartons to make a variety of different stencils.

2 Using a Medium Chalk Paint Brush, paint half the trunk in Chalk Paint in Chicago Grey and the other half in Oxford Navy. These are your base colours. Allow them to dry before starting the stencilling.

3 In your first layer of stencilling, start with the largest stencil shape and use a Chalk Paint Roller to layer the base colours on top of each other. Don't press too hard or the paint will bleed. Leave to dry (you can speed the drying process by using a hairdryer).

4 Interchange the remaining stencils to add your accent colours: Old Violet, Greek Blue and Old Ochre. Start with the darkest colour first, building up to your lighter colours.

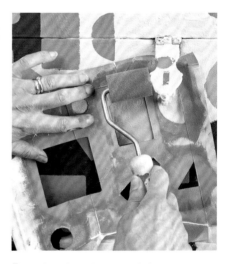

5 Overlap the colours and shapes. Make sure you allow the paint to dry in between each colour. You will find the Tetra Pak® is a little thicker than other stencils, but it is easy to wipe clean between coats. Leave to dry.

6 Seal the painted surface by taking a small amount of Clear Chalk Paint Wax and applying it with a Chalk Paint Wax Brush. This will protect your trunk and make it easier to wipe down.

Napoleonic Blue

Laminate Cabinet

One of my frequently asked questions is 'Can I paint laminate?' The answer is a definite YES! Chalk Paint has exceptional sticking power and so you can easily transform boring shiny laminate furniture into your own work of art.

You can find laminate furniture anywhere – from Ikea chest of drawers to mid-century kitchen cabinets and more. I found this 1960s-style cupboard online. It has great legs and is an interesting shape, but it was not looking its best with scratches and some crackled areas.

I wanted to give this piece a smooth finish and paint it with geometric shapes inspired by the American abstract minimalist artist Frank Stella, who died while I was making this book. I discovered his work when I was at art college and loved his use of colour, shaped canvases and minimalist approach to art.

On the wall and skirting/baseboard: Wall Paint in Napoleonic Blue

On the floor: Chalk Paint in Antibes Green

YOU WILL NEED

Sanding Pads (optional)

Chalk Paint in Napoleonic Blue, Emperor's Silk, Antibes Green, Arles and Tilton

Chalk Paint Brushes

Painter's masking tape

Hairdryer (optional)

Clear Chalk Paint Wax or Chalk Paint Lacquer

Chalk Paint Wax Brush, roller or spray gun

1 If the laminate you're painting is really shiny, sand it down lightly. This ensures that the paint has a textured surface to adhere to. Apply a thin coat of Chalk Paint in Napoleonic Blue. Feather the paint as you go to minimize brush strokes (see tip).

2 Make sure you leave plenty of time for your first coat to dry. Laminate isn't as absorbent as wood, so it will take longer than usual. Then add a second coat and leave to dry again.

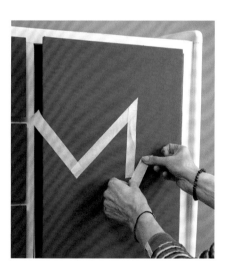

3 Using low-tack masking tape for delicate surfaces, mark out geometric shapes on your piece. Ensure the masking tape is pressed down firmly so the paint does not bleed.

4 Fill in the shapes with your chosen paint using a brush suitable for the size of the area you are painting. Remove the tape while the paint is still wet.

5 Once the paint is dry, mark out the next area with masking tape and apply the Chalk Paint.

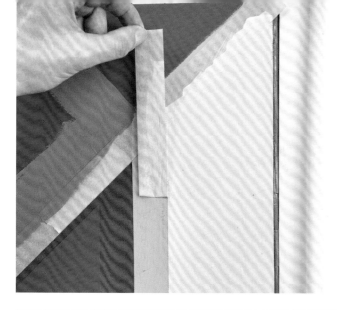

6 Repeat steps 4 and 5 until your pattern is complete, then immediately peel off the final layer of masking tape. You can use a hairdryer to speed up the drying process when painting your shapes.

7 Once your paint has dried, it's time to apply a protective coating. Choose Clear Chalk Paint Wax for a mellow finish or for extra durability, you could use Chalk Paint Lacquer, which can be applied with a brush, roller or even spray gun.

Amsterdam Green   Duck Egg Blue

Swedish Posy Decoupage Bureau

Bureaus are the best kept upcycling furniture secret and there's always one to be found in secondhand markets. They may seem old fashioned, but they are great for a home office as they can be used to hide away a laptop and for storage, too.

My favourite approach is to decorate them quietly on the outside and make them a riot on the inside. This simple bureau was given a stylish update using Chalk Paint in Amsterdam Green on the outside and Duck Egg Blue on the inside with the Swedish Posy Decoupage Paper I designed for Redesign with Prima.

Swedish Posy is a pretty floral pattern inspired by old Swedish painted interiors and has such a delicate sense of vintage romance, yet still feels contemporary. It was inspired by my travels to Sweden, where I visited many country homes. During the Gustavian era, country manor houses were often decorated in a restrained French-inspired Rococo style with delicate floral and bird motifs, muted pastel colours and delicate, carved wooden mouldings.

I love the cool dark green outside with the pretty and playful interior.

YOU WILL NEED

Chalk Paint in Amsterdam Green and Duck Egg Blue

Small Chalk Paint Brush

Painter's masking tape

Metal ruler

Pencil

Paper for templates

Scissors

A1 Decoupage Paper – we used my Annie Sloan x Redesign With Prima Swedish Posy

Image Medium

Small Flat Brush

Clear Chalk Paint Wax

Small Chalk Paint Wax Brush

Lint-free cloth

Cardboard/cardstock

On the wall: Wall Paint in Pointe Silk
On the skirting/baseboard: Chalk Paint in Old Ochre

1 Using a Chalk Paint Brush, paint your piece of furniture using Chalk Paint in Amsterdam Green on the outside and Duck Egg on the inside. Duck Egg is one of the harmony hues chosen to work with the Swedish Posy Decoupage Paper.

2 Use masking tape to create clean lines where the two paint colours meet.

3 Making paper templates is the best way to accurately apply Decoupage Paper to furniture with awkward and unusual shapes like this bureau. Cut out templates for the areas you are going to decoupage using a pencil and metal ruler. When you are happy with your templates, use them to cut out the areas of the Decoupage Paper design you want to apply to your piece.

4 Next, apply a coat of Image Medium to the areas of the bureau you are going to use decoupage paper on, using a Small Flat Brush. This acts as an adhesive to stick the Decoupage Paper to the inside of the bureau. Lay the Decoupage Paper on the surface. Press firmly and smooth from the centre outwards.

5 Apply another coat of Image Medium on top using a Small Flat Brush to seal the paper. Seal the rest of the bureau with Clear Chalk Paint Wax. Remove excess with a lint-free cloth.

6 To frame and finish off the Decoupage Paper area of the bureau, draw a line of Amsterdam Green around it using a length of cardboard as a ruler (or see tip below right).

TOP TIP You could mark out the painted border in step 6 with masking tape, but that will give a very sharp edge. Using cardboard gives a softer, more hand-drawn look.

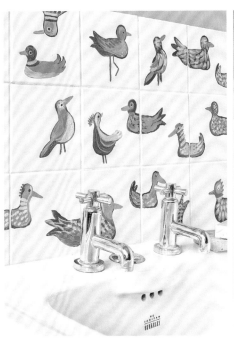

Weekend Projects

Get really stuck into a larger project over a weekend.
Try out more complex techniques and create a statement
piece that will define the look of the room, such as
a painted floor, a bed coronet or a window border.

Gilded French Sofa

YOU WILL NEED

Detail Brush Set

Gold Size

Loose Metal Leaf Booklets
in Imitation Gold

Chalk Paint (optional)

Small Chalk Paint Brush (optional)

Clear Chalk Paint Wax

Small Chalk Paint Wax Brush

Lint-free cloth

It's hard to believe, but this beauty of a sofa was extremely battered when I first spotted it in a flea market in France many years ago. It has since been reupholstered in my Antoinette + Old White Linen Union fabric and I painted the frame with Chalk Paint in Paris Grey. It has been in my son Felix's house for many years, but he's changing his style. As a result, I have claimed it back to give it a refresh and imbue it with some old-world glamour.

Reproduction French canapé sofas come in a variety of shapes and styles. They can be found in sales and auctions relatively inexpensively, although they may need reupholstering. They all have carving on the frame to a greater or lesser extent – from extravagant shell-like designs with scrolls, to delicate flowers and leaves – and they all look great when gilded.

The finished effect will look fabulously gold, but in fact I am using brass leaf, an imitation gold that, once waxed, is the exact same colour as real gold leaf. The real thing is very hard to use and very expensive, so brass is a very good alternative. Use loose rather than transfer leaf, as it will be easier to manipulate. Patience is needed, so get stuck in with a good podcast or some music and take your time.

On the wall: Wall Paint in Pointe Silk
On the skirting/baseboard: Chalk Paint in Old Ochre

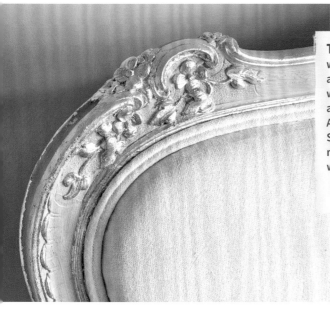

TOP TIP Gold Size is water-based and has the advantage of staying sticky when dry, so it's perfect for applying Loose Metal Leaf. Apply a thin layer of Gold Size and leave it for 3–7 minutes until it turns from white to clear.

1 Using a small pointed Detail Brush, paint Gold Size on the raised flower and leaf shapes and the scrolls of the sofa moulding. It is white when you first apply it but dries clear and shiny. If the surface is very absorbent, you will need to apply two coats. Wash your brush immediately after using Gold Size – it will dry hard! Leave it to dry on the sofa moulding for a few minutes and it will be ready to use. The Gold Size has to be sticky, not too wet or dry.

2 Before applying your Loose Metal Leaf, you need to make sure your hands are clean and dry and have no traces of Gold Size on them. Take a leaf from your booklet and tear it into smaller pieces to make it easier to use.

3 Use a flat Detail Brush to press the Loose Metal Leaf down onto your piece. It doesn't matter which side faces up. Use a dabbing movement to press it into place. Press the leaf into all the crevices. If you miss bits, don't worry; you can go over them again. Don't panic if it looks a mess, it will all come together in the end!

4 Sweep off all the excess Loose Metal Leaf quite forcefully using your Detail Brush. This is to make sure everything is stuck down, but also to remove any excess where you didn't paint Gold Size.

5 You will be able to see how the piece is looking at this stage and add more Gold Size and Loose Metal Leaf to any areas you have missed. If you have Gold Size where you don't want it, you can paint it out using Chalk Paint and a Small Chalk Paint Brush.

6 Once you are happy with your gilding, seal the sofa moulding with Clear Chalk Paint Wax. Remove excess with a lint-free cloth.

French Linen

Diamond Chequerboard Floor

This diamond chequerboard floor was painted at Court House Farm in Portishead, England over a previously painted surface. This wonderful venue is where I hold my Painting Retreats in the UK. Here we have recreated the design step by step on a board to demonstrate the technique.

The old paintwork had begun to wear away, so we devised this wonderful chequerboard design using the contrast of flat and even paint with the original texture. It immediately updated the room with minimum fuss. Many people have similarly time-worn painted floors in their homes, so this is a great way to work with what you have. Diamonds or squares are easy to paint and look good in any style of house – modern or old.

Planning beforehand, clearing the room and working out the scale of the pattern are very important. I find marking out with string and some Blu Tack® is really helpful at this stage. Always design the chequerboard pattern from the centre, bearing in mind how it will look around a main feature in the room such as a doorway or fireplace. We chose a colour that is close in tone to the original floor colour, but a darker colour would create a very striking contrast.

YOU WILL NEED

Sanding Pads

Clear Matt Chalk Paint Lacquer

Roller

Scissors

String

Blu Tack®

Long metal ruler

Pencil

Chalk Paint in French Linen

Small Flat Brush

TOP TIP If you are worried about painting freehand, you can use painter's masking tape to mark out your pattern and paint the shapes. However, this is quite wasteful and can often take longer – and it's easy to get confused and find you've painted the wrong side of the tape!

1 Prepare the surface to create as smooth a finish as possible. Make sure the floor is clean and dry. Sand it lightly to remove any loose paint and seal it with Chalk Paint Lacquer using a roller, then leave to dry.

2 Find the centre of the floor by cutting two pieces of string long enough to extend from one corner to the opposite corner. Use some Blu Tack® to hold them in place. Where they cross is the centre point.

3 Decide what size you want the square or diamond pattern to be. Using string, Blu Tack® and a ruler, mark out your grid of shapes on the floor as shown. Then use a pencil and a long steel ruler to draw over the string lines. You should have a perfect grid over your whole floor.

4 Paint in your diamond shapes with Chalk Paint in French Linen using a Small Flat Brush. Use the straight edge of the brush to get a crisp line.

5 Freehand painting your squares give a softer, more pleasing effect and once you get going is much quicker than using masking tape.

6 Fill in the diamond shapes with paint and leave to dry, then apply a second coat. Once the paint has dried, apply two coats of Chalk Paint Lacquer to seal the floor. This will prevent scuffs and scratches and makes cleaning easier. Make sure the paint is dry and your floors are clean before this to ensure no dust or debris gets trapped under the sealant.

Dutch Folk Art Shoe Lasts

YOU WILL NEED

Chalk Paint in Louis Blue, Giverny, Old White, Oxford Navy and Country Grey

Chalk Paint Brush

MixMat (optional)

Pencil

Small bowls or plastic containers

Detail Brush Set

Clear Chalk Paint Wax

Lint-free cloth

I have seen wooden shoe lasts on sale in flea markets all over the world and wondered what I could do with them. It was when I was in one of my Chalk Paint stockists' shops in the Netherlands that the idea came to me. She had wooden lasts hanging near some beautiful Dutch folk art and I had the idea to combine the two.

Wooden shoe lasts are foot moulds upon which a bespoke shoe can be constructed. They were originally hand-carved by cordwainers (shoemakers) using hardwoods such as maple or beech. The shoemaker would take a customer's foot measurements and then carve a last that perfectly fitted them. They could then make them the perfect bespoke shoes again and again.

Victoria painted the beautiful designs for this project. We based the design on Hindelooper art, which is a type of traditional decorative painting originating in Friesland in the Netherlands. It was a form of folk art painted by the maritime community of Hinderloopen. During bad weather when the fishermen were stuck ashore, they would paint as a way to make some money. It is the art of people who weren't trained painters but liked making decorative patterns.

TOP TIP Plan out your design first, experimenting with colourways on paper. Folk art is a great place for inspiration and ideas. Rework traditional designs by using modern colours to give them a simpified and more contemporary look.

Louis Blue

Giverny

Oxford Navy

1. Apply two coats of Chalk Paint in Louis Blue to the shoe lasts and leave to dry after each coat. We painted the lasts on a MixMat, but this is optional.

2 Using a pencil, trace your design on to the shoe lasts to use as a guide before painting. You can copy the drawings shown here if you want to recreate this design.

3 We've used five harmonious paint colours for this design. Begin by diluting all your chosen colours with a splash of water in small bowls or plastic containers. With a Detail Brush, begin painting the base colour of the tulip flower design using Chalk Paint in Giverny.

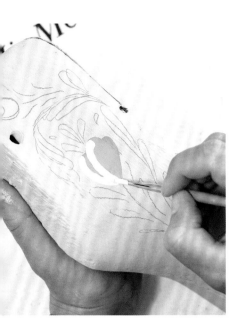

4 While the base layer is still slightly wet, add details from top to bottom using Chalk Paint in Old White so that the paint pulls.

5 Repeat step 4, using Chalk Paint in Oxford Navy to continue the flower design.

6 Paint the other elements of the design using Chalk Paint in Country Grey as the base, leaving to dry before you add the details in Oxford Navy and Old White. Seal with Clear Chalk Paint Wax using a lint-free cloth.

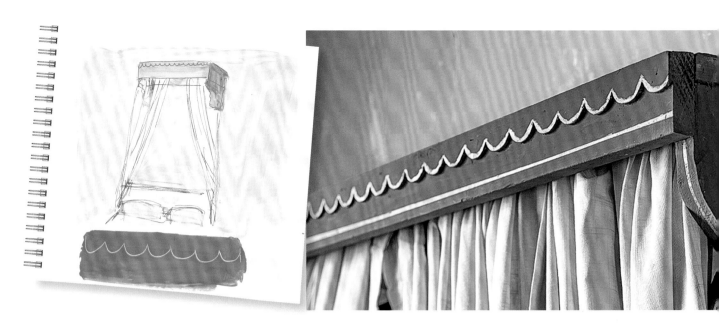

Bed Coronet

I have always loved coronets above beds, but vintage ones are rare and new ones are expensive. For some time I have been thinking of ways of making one myself. It's such an amazing way to make your bedroom look upscale and pretty.

My first thought was to find a secondhand console or demi-lune table and take the legs off. I looked for ages and couldn't find one, but then I stumbled on this bench (or is it a shelf?). What I thought was interesting was that it was quite shallow and had a lip at the front, so I could hide the fabric for the curtains inside.

It had been painted unevenly with gloss paint for a rough country effect, so I sanded it down and repainted it in a smooth flat finish ready for a more sophisticated look. I chose an elegant palette of blue and gold. Because the coronet will be up high and won't need to be cleaned, you don't need to wax it. Simply enjoy the lovely contrast between the matt Chalk Paint and the metallic Gilding Wax.

YOU WILL NEED

Sanding Pads

Chalk Paint in Aubusson Blue

Small Chalk Paint Brush

Painter's masking tape

Warm Gold and Bright Gold Gilding Wax

MixMat

Detail Brush Set

Aubusson Blue

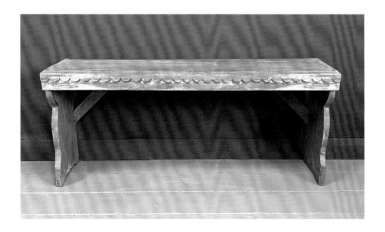

1 First remove any excess paint from your piece by rubbing it down with a coarse Sanding Pad to create a smooth surface. Using a Chalk Paint Brush, apply two coats of Chalk Paint in Aubusson Blue. Because the coronet will be elevated above a bed, you will need to paint the underside as well.

2 Use two strips of masking tape to create a thin line along the top of the shelf.

3 Using a Detail Brush, combine a little Warm Gold and Bright Gold Gilding Wax on a MixMat to create a blend of the two shades.

4 Spread alternating Warm Gold, Bright Gold and the mixed Gilding Wax evenly (and not too thickly) in small sections along the length of the masking tape.

5 Remove the masking tape promptly. You will be left with a lovely strip of metallic colour – the blended mix gives it a real shimmer.

6 Use a small square Detail Brush to pick out the decorative moulding in Gilding Wax by hand. Don't overload your brush and lean on your elbow to ensure a steady hand.

Faux Malachite Desk

Dress to impress using this eye-catching technique on your furniture! Malachite is an intensely coloured, semi-precious gemstone and is found on expensive antique pieces, often from Italy. It's glamorous, dramatic and elegant and usually accompanied by gold and black.

I found this desk in a secondhand furniture store and was immediately captivated by its strong but delicate shape. It is a good quality piece, but the shiny varnished surface had been damaged, so it was a perfect candidate for painting.

As faux malachite is strong in colour and pattern, a little goes a long way. For this reason, I chose to paint just the drawer fronts. It also needs to be done in small areas to keep the paint wet while you make the patterns and on a flat area rather than moulded. If you want to use this technique on a larger surface, divide the area into smaller geometric shapes using a pencil and ruler as a guide. This paint effect could alternatively be done on a very modern cube-shaped piece of furniture.

On the wall: Wall Paint in Primer Red
On the skirting/baseboard: Chalk Paint in Primer Red
On the floor: Satin Paint in French Linen

YOU WILL NEED

Satin Paint in Athenian Black

Small Flat Brushes

MixMat

Chalk Paint in Old White, Florence and Amsterdam Green

Sanding Pads

Chalk Paint Lacquer in Gloss

Cardboard/cardstock to rip up

Stencil Brush

Small Round Detail Brush

Florence

Amsterdam Green

1 Using a Small Flat Brush, paint the whole desk in two coats of Satin Paint in Athenian Black. Leave to dry.

2 On the MixMat, thoroughly mix 6 parts Chalk Paint in Old White to 1 part Chalk Paint in Florence. This will be your base colour for the malachite effect.

3 Remove the drawers and handles and apply two coats of the base colour to the drawer fronts. Use a small amount of paint and brush out as far as you can so there are no brush marks. Once dry, sand with a Fine Grade Sanding Pad.

4 Apply Chalk Paint Lacquer with another Small Flat Brush. Make sure there are no marks. Leave to dry.

5 Tear off a flap from a cardboard box. Fold it and tear along the fold to create a rectangular malachite pattern-making tool. Repeat this several times – you will need a good supply because the paint will absorb into the cardboard.

6 On the MixMat, combine Chalk Paint in Amsterdam Green with Gloss Chalk Paint Lacquer to create a pliable mixture. It needs to be translucent enough that you can see through the paint to the MixMat.

7 Apply the Amsterdam Green mix to a small area of the drawer front using the same Small Flat Brush that you used to create the mixture.

8 Create the malachite effect by wiggling and dragging the dry cardboard over the wet paint in a semi-circular motion. The torn edge of the cardboard is better than the smooth area to get the right effect.

9 Repeat steps 7 and 8 to cover all the drawer fronts one section at a time, working quickly before the mixture dries. When your cardboard becomes soggy, discard it and use a fresh piece.

TOP TIP Malachite is a strikingly beautiful emerald-green mineral, which adds a luxe touch when used in interiors. Real malachite tables are made in sections of square or triangular shapes. It may be helpful to look at photographs for inspiration before you begin this project.

10 Use a Stencil Brush to stipple out any dark areas and blur the joins while the paint is still wet.

11 Add depth and definition by drawing into the wet paint using the end of a Small Round Detail Brush.

12 Leave to dry, then sand with a Medium Sanding Pad and apply two coats of Chalk Paint Lacquer.

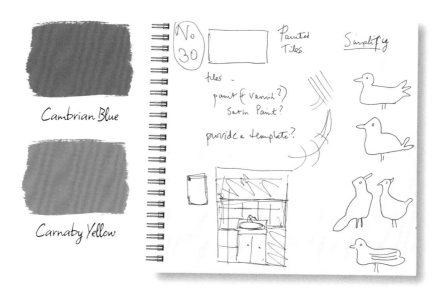

Cambrian Blue

Carnaby Yellow

Decorative Bird Tiles

This project was inspired by a bathroom painted by Devon-based contemporary artist Emily Powell (@emilypowellstudio on Instagram). Emily used Chalk Paint to transform the tiles in her small cloakroom with charming bird paintings. She says, 'Birds are that place between reality and dream world. The nearest beings to angels, ghosts and dinosaurs. I've painted them all over my tiles because their very beings bring me comfort.' I loved Emily's idea so much that I asked her if I could recreate it for this book.

I have drawn some ducks and seagulls for you to use as templates (see page 171). You can photocopy and resize them so they fit your tiles, or create your own designs for this project. Prep your tiles carefully by cleaning them with sugar soap to get rid of any dirt or grease. These decorative tiles are not designed to withstand heavy cleaning.

YOU WILL NEED

Sugar soap

Lint-free cloth

Paper and pencil

Carbon paper

Painter's masking tape

Satin Paint in Cambrian Blue, Oxford Navy, Carnaby Yellow and Old White

Detail Brush Set

On the wall: Wall Paint in Pemberley Blue

On the stool: Chalk Paint in Barcelona Orange

TOP TIP Remove any carbon marks from the tiles using a soft eraser after the paint has dried. Avoid scrubbing at your design and don't use bleach or harsh cleaning products. If you use a soft wet cloth on your tiles, your design should last. You can apply Chalk Paint Lacquer for additional protection, if you like.

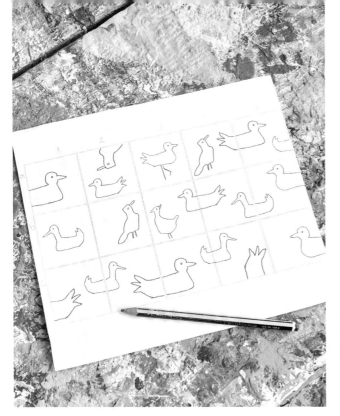

1 Before painting directly onto the tiles, sketch out a plan on a piece of paper. It doesn't have to be perfect – just a useful tool to help place the birds and plan your colour scheme.

2 Increase or decrease the scale of the bird template designs (see page 171) on a photocopier so that they fit the size of your tiles.

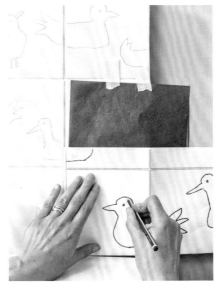

3 Lay a sheet of carbon paper on one of the tiles, carbon-side down, and affix with masking tape. Place the template on top and use a pencil to trace around the bird design, pressing firmly. Remove the template and carbon paper to reveal the duck design now transferred to your tile. Repeat for the remaining tiles, using a new sheet of carbon paper each time.

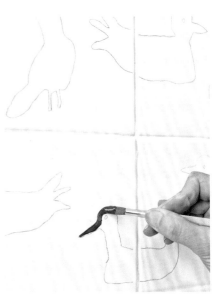

4 Using the carbon lines as a guide, paint the birds onto your chosen tiles. Start with a base colour and paint the outlines first.

5 Fill in the outlines, still using the base colour. Allow for drying time between different colours to prevent the paints becoming muddy.

6 When the base coat is dry, you can re-apply the bird design using a new piece of carbon paper and draw in the beak, eyes and feathers. With the carbon marks to guide you, this makes it easy to paint the smaller details. Leave to dry, then erase the carbon marks (see tip on page 151).

Tudor Style Window Border

Court House Farm in Somerset is the setting for my UK Painting Retreats, so I am a regular visitor to this much-loved and magical place. Its owner Helen Reed was keen to add some decorative painting to the interior of the house, so I began to plan something for this book.

The farm is steeped in history, having started as a medieval house in the 1300s that developed into a Tudor manor in the 16th century. Helen's colour scheme for the house has various earthy pinks and ochres. However, she also loves modern design, so I wanted my design to reflect that.

I researched early English wall painting looking for inspiration and discovered the wonderful Elizabethan examples at Ledbury in Herefordshire, which were painted in the 1560s or 1570s. I was amazed to see a design with elements that seem so modern and relatable despite being painted so long ago. Even the colour palette of earthy pinks, ochre yellow, black, grey and white hit the mark! I did lots of sketches and came up with the idea for this window border.

I began by painting the wall in Piranesi Pink and then painted my border in roughly, using a long plank of wood to keep everything in a straight line. The first two attempts went completely wrong, as I had made the design far too big, so both times I painted over it with Piranesi Pink and started again.

YOU WILL NEED

Wall Paint in Piranesi Pink

Wall Paint Brush

Chalk Paint in Arles, Scandinavian Pink, Primer Red, Barcelona Orange, Original and Graphite

Paper

Small Flat Brush

Detail Brush Set

Pencil

Scissors

Plank of wood

Sanding Pads

Scandinavian Pink

Arles

1 Paint the wall with Wall Paint in Piranesi Pink and leave to dry. Once you have found the correct scale, make a final Chalk Paint sketch of your design on paper using a Small Flat Brush and Detail Brush Set. Take a pencil and a fresh sheet of paper and draw templates for each shape, then cut these out with scissors.

2 Using a long plank of wood as a guide, draw a straight pencil line vertically on either side of the window to mark where the inner edge of the border will be.

3 Use the pencil lines to align the templates on the wall. Paint round them loosely so that the shapes aren't completely uniform.

4 Whenever you need to paint a straight line, use the plank as a guide for your brush.

5 If you like, you can blend some of the Chalk Paint colours with Wall Paint in Piranesi Pink. Including these blended shades in your design will make sure everything looks cohesive together.

6 Using the Small Flat Brush and Detail Brush Set, build up the layers of your design.

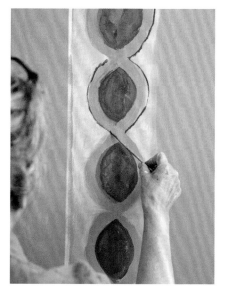

7 Hold the brushes loosely to get an 'evenly uneven' look.

8 Add the finishing touches to the window border.

9 Add some painted decoration underneath the window as well, then leave to dry completely.

10 Sand the wall lightly with a coarse Sanding Pad to give it a worn, slightly faded look.

Duck Egg Blue   Amsterdam Green

Trompe-l'œil Cabinet

Trompe-l'œil means 'deceive the eye' in French and is a technique that makes painted objects appear realistic and three-dimensional. This looks very complicated and difficult to do, but here Joanna shows how simple it is!

These painted panels are merely a series of lines in varying tones. It was a common way for Victorians to make basic furniture made out of deal look more expensive. This piece was a old TV cabinet, but we have restyled it as a pretty laundry cupboard.

Using a mid-tone for the base colour ensures you have a good contrast of mid, light and dark tones working together. By using your dark tones (lowlights) and light tones (highlights) opposite each other on either side of a drawer or cupboard door, you can achieve a 3D quality. Imagine the sun coming in from one direction, lighting up one side and casting a shadow on the other. If you're unsure, do a quick sketch with a pencil beforehand to determine where the light and shadow will go.

YOU WILL NEED

Chalk Paint in Duck Egg Blue, Amsterdam Green, Graphite and Pure

Chalk Paint Brushes

MixMat

Detail Brush Set

Clear Chalk Paint Wax

Chalk Paint Wax Brush

Lint-free cloth

On the wall: Wall Paint in Cambrian Blue
On the skirting/baseboard: Chalk Paint in Aubusson Blue
On the floor: Satin Paint in French Linen

TOP TIP Use your little finger to guide you around the edge of the furniture. This will help keep your hand steady as the paint flows from your brush. It's important to get the ratio of paint to water right – it should be the consistency of single cream/light cream, so that it flows from your brush smoothly. Let the paint flow from your brush until it runs out and then repeat to create a fluid join. Look ahead and not down at the paintbrush.

1 If your piece has drawers, take them out to paint. Apply two coats of Chalk Paint in Duck Egg Blue all over using a Large Chalk Paint Brush and let it dry completely after each coat.

2 On a MixMat, make a mid-tone colour by mixing one part Chalk Paint in Amsterdam Green to four parts Duck Egg Blue. Using a Flat Detail Brush, paint a stripe around the drawers and doors the same thickness as the brush. This will register as a raised area. Don't worry if your lines are a little wobbly, as this adds character to the piece.

3 Using a Small Round Detail Brush, paint your lowlights using Chalk Paint in Graphite along the base and side edges of the mid-tone stripe, using the same method as in step 2. If you're unsure, imagine the sun coming from the top right and casting a shadow.

4 Wash your Small Round Detail Brush and repeat the process but this time using Chalk Paint in Pure to create highlights. These should be opposite your lowlights on either side of a drawer or cupboard door.

5 When you have completed all your highlights and lowlights, let the paint dry completely before sealing it with Clear Chalk Paint Wax. This will protect the piece and create a durable surface. Buff out the wax with a lint-free cloth.

Coolabah Green

Antoinette

Charleston Inspired Headboard

YOU WILL NEED

Chalk Paint in Coolabah Green, Svenska Blue, Honfleur, Aubusson Blue, Capri Pink, Paprika Red and Antoinette

Small Chalk Paint Brush

MixMat

Mixing Stick

Detail Brush Set

Clear Chalk Paint Wax

Small Chalk Paint Wax Brush

We probably all have a piece of yellowish orange pine furniture from the 1970s or 80s in our homes and they can be found in every secondhand furniture store. They are often useful, practical and well-made pieces, but they look dated because of the colour.

This headboard is one of these pieces! I could have just painted it white, but I wanted to show you how to turn it into something completely unique by adding some colour and pattern.

The colours and motifs are inspired by Charleston, the famous English living museum of art and design in Sussex. The Bloomsbury Group artists who lived at Charleston loved to emphasize the character of the furniture and the rooms they were working with and used repeat graphic shapes, botanical motifs and lots and lots of colour. My doodles are organic and in response to the shape and look of this headboard. It's good to be relaxed when you are painting in this style – kick off your shoes, put on some music or a good podcast, zone out and let the creativity flow.

1 Paint the pine headboard with Chalk Paint in Coolabah Green using a Small Chalk Paint Brush. Pine is quite absorbent, so you will need two coats. Leave it to dry.

2 Create a Charleston-inspired blue on the MixMat by mixing Chalk Paint in Svenska Blue, Honfleur and Aubusson Blue. Separately, mix together Chalk Paint in Capri Pink and Paprika Red. Finally, place some Chalk Paint in Antoinette on the MixMat. These are the three colours you will use to create your design.

3 Add plenty of water to some of your blue Chalk Paint mix. Using a Mixing Stick and a Detail Brush, mark out a loose grid of blue dots on the central panel of the headboard. Start by creating the four points of a square and then add a dot in the middle.

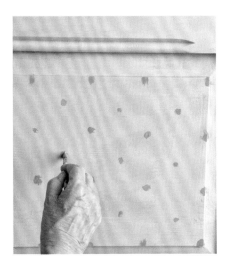

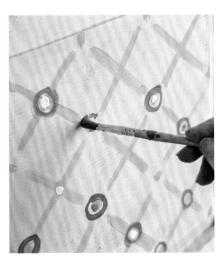

4 Painting the dots by eye, rather than with a ruler, gives a fluid look to the grid.

5 Holding a Detail Brush at one end, draw crosses from corner to corner of your squares.

6 At the centre of each grid point, paint random dots, some in Chalk Paint in Antoinette and others in the pink Chalk Paint mix. Circle the dots using the undiluted blue Chalk Paint mix. Don't worry about it all looking perfect. Focus on the bigger picture rather than the detail – it will come together at the end.

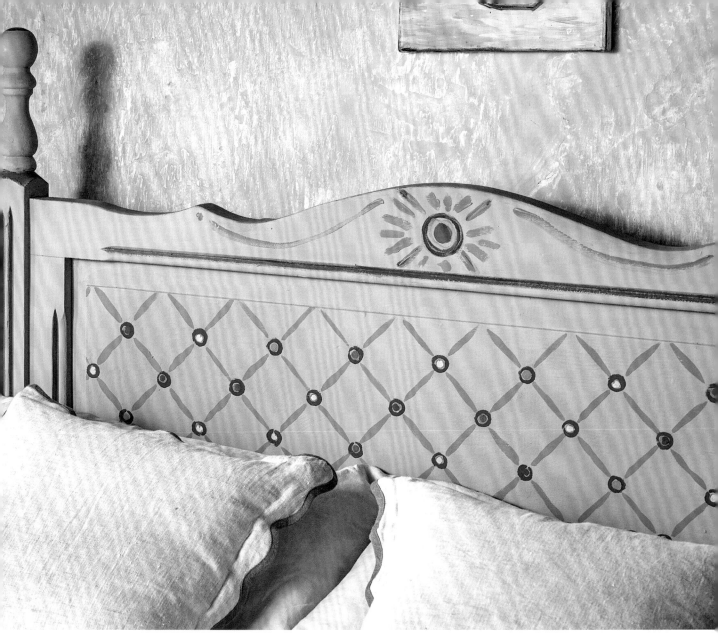

7 This headboard had grooves down each side so I used these as guides to draw four lines of each colour down both sides. Add a little water to the Chalk Paint and pull the brush down the line, letting it do the work. Don't hold it like a pencil and you will find you produce beautifully natural, fluid lines. I also added some decoration to the top of the headboard (see above). Leave to dry, then seal the headboard with Clear Chalk Paint Wax using a Small Chalk Paint Wax Brush.

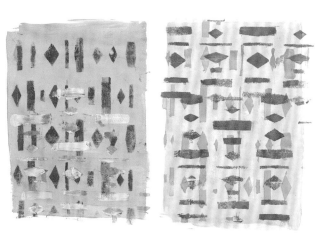

Paper Cut-Out
Filing Cabinet

Filing cabinets are so often found in secondhand stores, but they may not speak to us because they are so big and bulky. Now that many of us are working from home, we do need somewhere to keep papers and more.

This metal filing cabinet lives in my workshop and it's where I keep all my many sketchbooks. I wanted it to transform it into something lively and inspiring to look at so that it wouldn't be just a near-invisible presence in the corner.

The inspiration for the design came from my visit to Santa Fe in New Mexico. The surrounding countryside, the former home of artist Georgia O'Keeffe and the Museum of International Folk Art offered up so many wonderful colour combinations.

I decided on a paper cut-out stencil technique to make an abstract design. It's simply folding and cutting a geometric design out of paper to make a stencil. You may remember this cutting technique from making paper snowflakes as a child. We're simply turning the snowflake into a stencil. The design, coupled with the right colours, has transformed this cabinet into something I am proud to have in my studio.

YOU WILL NEED

Large Sponge Roller

MixMat

Chalk Paint in Paprika Red, Florence, Arles and Old White

Cartridge paper

Craft knife or scissors

Pencil

Painter's masking tape

Small Sponge Roller

Chalk Paint Lacquer in Matt

On the wall: Wall Paint in Napoleonic Blue

On the skirting/baseboard: Chalk Paint in Napoleonic Blue

On the floor: Chalk Paint in Antibes Green

On the desk: Chalk Paint in Louis Blue

On the chair: Chalk Paint in Paprika Red

Paprika Red

Florence

1 Using a Large Sponge Roller and MixMat, paint the whole filing cabinet in two coats of Chalk Paint in Paprika Red. Apply the paint in different directions to create a patterned finish and give the smooth surface of the filing cabinet more character and movement.

2 To create your stencil, it is best to use thick cartridge paper that won't disintegrate when covered in paint. Cut a piece of paper to the same width as your filing cabinet and fold into four. Cut out your stencil design along the folded edges.

3 When finished, create a dupicate stencil by drawing around it using a pencil and cutting it out with a craft knife or scissors. You will end up with two stencils exactly the same – one for each colour.

TIP You could make more than one duplicate of your stencil because if you are using it multiple times it can get a bit soggy and disintegrate. It's easier to do this right at the beginning than halfway through!

4 We painted the cabinet upright, but you might want to lay it on a blanket on its side to make it easier to work. Using masking tape, stick your stencil onto the cabinet in the position you want. Use plenty of masking tape to ensure it won't move when you apply the paint with the roller.

5 Load up a Small Sponge Roller with Chalk Paint in Florence and roller over the cut-out stencil. If the paint doesn't reach every part of the stencil, don't worry – the mottled effect adds depth to the piece. Remove the stencil and allow the paint to dry.

6 Create a mix of Chalk Paint in Arles and Old White on the MixMat. Use about 70% Arles and 30% Old White. This mix ensure the colours look less flat and shimmer slightly.

7 Stick the second paper cut-out stencil in the opposite direction to the first one using masking tape. Load up the Small Sponge Roller with your Chalk Paint colour mix and roller over the stencil. Remove the stencil.

8 Once all your paint is dry, use the Large Sponge Roller to apply Chalk Paint Lacquer over the whole surface. This will provide a heavy-duty finish to your filing cabinet.

Templates

Reverse Stencilled Chest (pages 78–81)

Decorative Bird Tiles (pages 150–153)

Resources

Preloved furniture is fun to find, kind to the environment and can save you a lot of money. Vintage pieces are often well made and will add a unique touch to your home. Keep the key measurements of your space and a tape measure with you at all times and you'll always be ready to snap up a bargain.

Here are some of the best places to buy preloved furniture.

Flea Markets/Brocantes

Flea markets are great places to find a large number of vendors all in one place. Different countries have different names for flea markets.

In the US they can be called swap meets. In Australia they are trash and treasure markets. In France and Belgium they are called marchés aux puces (literally 'flea markets'), brocantes or vide-greniers. In Germany, the most common word is Flohmarkt and in the Netherlands it is vlooienmarkt.

The best way to find a local flea market is good old Google, although FleaMapket (www.fleamapket.com) lists markets in lots of different countries.

You can find more information on US markets from The National Flea Market Association (www.fleamarkets.org).

France has amazing brocantes all year round. Pick up a little yellow book called L'Agenda des Brocantes (www.agendadesbrocantes.fr) at a local supermarket – it lists all the brocantes in the region by date and town.

You can also search for local brocantes on www.brocabrac.fr and www.vide-greniers.org. For brocantes in Belgium, try www.visitwallonia.com for an up-to-date list.

Antiques Markets

All over the world there are amazing antiques markets, where you will find higher quality furniture to paint.

In the UK, the International Antique & Collectors Fairs (www.iacf.co.uk) lists most of the larger ones such as Ardlingly, Newark, Shepton Mallet, Stoneleigh and Newbury.

Other great markets include:

Sunbury Antiques Market at Kempton Park Racecourse
www.sunburyantiques.com

The Great Antiques & Vintage Fair at Wetherby Racecourse
www.jaguarfairs.com

Antiques & Home Show at Lincoln Showground
www.asfairs.com

In the US there are some famous big antiques markets, including:

The Rose Bowl Flea Market in Pasadena, CA
www.rgcshows.com

Brimfield Antique Flea Market in Brimfield, MA
www.brimfieldantiquefleamarket.com

The Original Round Top Antiques Fair in Round Top, TX
www.roundtoptexasantiques.com

Brooklyn Flea in Brooklyn, NY
www.brooklynflea.com

Junk Shops

Every town has a junk shop selling used furniture at cheap prices. Some of them specialize in home clearances. Get to know the people who run your local shop and tell them what you are looking for. They may even call you when something they think you might be interested comes in.

Car Boot Sales

Car boot sales are popular in the United Kingdom, but they are also a common sight in parts of Australia and have a growing presence in mainland Europe. They usually take place in the summer months in large outdoor locations such as car parks or fields. Check your local newspaper or community website for dates and locations. Remember that you will need a car to get there and to transport your purchases home.

Charity Shops

Charity shops may also be referred to as thrift stores in the US and Canada, or as hospice shops, resale shops or opportunity (or op) shops in Australia and New Zealand.

Most big charities such as Oxfam, Dorothy House, Sue Ryder, Emmaus and the British Heart Foundation have special furniture stores where the bigger pieces go.

Auction Houses

The more intrepid shoppers bid online at auctions and salerooms. Sign up for newsletter alerts to find out when they are in your area. Don't be afraid of auction rooms – the staff will always help explain the bidding process and you can often view and buy ahead of the auction itself.

Local Finds

Don't forget to keep an eye out for people leaving things outside their houses to take, skips/dumpsters (but check before taking anything) and local recycling depots. Friends and family are also often great resources for old pieces of furniture they no longer have a place for.

eBay

www.ebay.co.uk
www.ebay.com

The original online auction site where you can find almost anything, although you may have to be patient, as there is a lot to scroll through.

Facebook Marketplace

www.facebook.com/marketplace

This is a free-to-use e-commerce platform that connects sellers and buyers. It is a good place to find furniture at bargain prices. You have to sign up to Facebook, and then you can search within your local area or nationwide – keep in mind that this may result in higher delivery costs.

Gumtree

www.gumtree.com

Gumtree started out in 2000 as a community site for people who had recently moved to London from Australia, New Zealand and South Africa, and was used to find flat shares, jobs and friends. Nowadays, Gumtree is the #1 online classified advertisement site in the UK and is available in over 60 countries.

Classified ads are either free or paid for depending on the product category and the geographical market. Gumtree is perfect for bigger items that can't easily be posted. As a buyer, you can target sellers specifically in your area and then go and collect the item.

PreLoved

www.preloved.co.uk

Preloved began in 1998 and has grown to become one of the largest classified advertising sites in the UK with hundreds of thousands of adverts in over 500 categories. With over 10 million members, Preloved has no listing fees, no selling fees and you can upgrade your account to get extra benefits for as little as £5 a year. There is even a Freeloved section, where you will find adverts from people who are giving items away for no cost.

Vinterior

www.vinterior.co

Vinterior is an online marketplace where you can buy and sell pre-loved furniture and homeware. There are 2,000 sellers from over 30 countries, so it's easy to find one-of-a-kind pieces and shop in a way that's better for the planet. From mid-century modern to traditional antiques, Vinterior sells good quality pieces.

Selency

www.selency.co.uk

Selency is a similar concept to Vinterior, but based in France – so you can find all those brocante buys from the comfort of your sofa.

The Saleroom

www.the-saleroom.com

The Saleroom is an online platform for physical auctions taking place around the UK and worldwide. You can set alerts for things you are looking for and get notified when they come up for sale.

Narchie

www.narchie.com

Narchie is a social marketplace for homewares, where decor enthusiasts can buy, sell and connect. It brings together smaller sellers, so it's a bit easier to navigate than eBay. Download the Narchie app from your app store.

Freecycle

www.freecycle.org

The Freecycle network is made up of more than 5,000 local Town groups with over 11 million members across the globe. It's a grassroots and entirely nonprofit movement of people who are giving (and getting) stuff for free in their own towns and keeping good pieces out of landfills. Membership is free – you join one or more local groups, post about things you want to give or receive, other members reply and you arrange a pickup time and location.

Craigslist

www.craigslist.org

Craigslist was founded in 1995 in San Francisco. It is a classified advertisement website where you can search for furniture. The site is now used in 570 cities in 70 countries, so you can find preloved items close to home.

Instagram

www.instagram.com

Follow secondhand furniture dealers on Instagram. Many dealers list pieces on their feeds and you just DM or comment to buy an item. You have to keep checking back to bag a bargain, but if you find a dealer whose style you like, send a message and explain what you are looking for – you might get first refusal on the perfect piece. To help you get started, search for hashtags such as #usedfurniture, #secondhandfurniture, #vintagefurniture, #secondhand, #upcycledfurniture and #reusedfurniture.

Index

Picture Credits

All artworks by Annie Sloan, copyright ©
Annie Sloan.

All photography by Jesse Wild, copyright ©
CICO Books unless otherwise stated below.

Key: Ph = photographer; a = above;
b = below; l = left; c = centre; r = right.

10–15 Ph Andrew Wood © CICO Books;

28 Ph © Polly Wreford at
www.sarahkaye.com

31 Ph Jesse Wild © Annie Sloan

36 Ph Jesse Wild © Annie Sloan

37 Ph © Polly Wreford at
www.sarahkaye.com

38–43 Ph Jesse Wild © Annie Sloan

61 r: Ph Jesse Wild © Annie Sloan

62: Ph Jesse Wild © Annie Sloan

63 al, ac, bl & bc: Ph Jesse Wild
© Annie Sloan

Acknowledgments

This book would not have been possible without the help of a great many people! More than any other book I've written, I've had to enlist help from others so I could get everything painted alongside my increasingly busy work schedule.

My thanks go first to the Annie Sloan team at my warehouse in Oxford, England, who work tirelessly behind the scenes, sourcing furniture, booking photoshoots, painting backdrops, finding props, making coffee and so much more. On this book, I'd like to thank Rachel Davis, my head of design, for being the spreadsheet queen and keeping us all on track, together with her design team, Gemma Hattersley Pitt and Joanna Lloyd, for doing visual research, working on projects and providing sketches and templates for the book. Thank you to our social media manager, Victoria Hopcroft, for her beautiful painting work on some of the projects. Thank you to Katherine Raderecht, my brand director, who helped plan and organize the photoshoots, worked on the text and has been the main point of contact for the team at CICO Books.

Special thanks go to Jesse Wild (@wildjesse), my amazing photographer, who took all the photographs in this book. Jesse is the king of lighting. He has a wonderful eye, works tirelessly to get the perfect shot and also provides the most wonderful soundtrack to all our shoots with his incredible taste in music. His humour and patience also keep us all sane when the pressure is on.

Thank you to Sophie Brown (@curated_calm) who was my main 'prep' painter on this book. She helped prepare many of the pieces of furniture for me – from sourcing them to taking them to pieces, sanding them down and painting base coats. She also painted most of the walls and floors you see in each shot and assisted on all the photoshoots. Thank you too to my PA, Rachel Munday, who kept us fed and watered and my diary free when I needed to work on the book.

Thanks to my amazing general manager, Tanya Janko, who works hard behind the scenes to make sure everything runs smoothly when I am focused on my book.

Thank you to Helen Reed and Mick Kreczmer at Court House Farm (@courthousefarm) in Portishead near Bristol, for allowing us to use their beautiful medieval house as a location for this book. We also run our UK retreats there, so I know this fabulous couple well. They welcomed the whole team with open arms and even helped with drilling, sewing and painting for us.

Many thanks to Tristan Merriam (@dogheaddesigns) and Jonathon Marc Mendes (@jonathonmarcmendes_paintedlove) for providing projects for the book. Thanks also to Cathie Wood from MadeByMeXStudio (@madebymeeex) for her help with inspiration and wooden bowls, and to The Art Of Pátina Antiques (@the.art. of.patina.antiques) and Emily Powell (@emilypowellstudio) for providing inspiration for some of the projects.

Thank you to the team at CICO Books. Annabel Morgan, senior commissioning editor; Sally Powell, art director; Sophie Devlin, editor; Gordana Simakovic, production manager; and Danielle Rawlings, editorial assistant.

Finally, thanks to my husband, David, for his support throughout the whole process. I couldn't do it without you!

Follow me
For more information about Annie Sloan Interiors and for a complete list of stockists where you can buy my Chalk Paint and other products, please go to:
www.anniesloan.com

For inspiration, find me on:
Instagram: *@AnnieSloanHome,*
@ChalkPaint, @AnnieSloanstagram
Facebook: *www.facebook.com/AnnieSloanHome*
YouTube: *www.youtube.com/AnnieSloanHome*
Pinterest: *www.pinterest.com/AnnieSloanHome*